ALL BLACK STUDENTS MEET

ALL BLACK STUDENTS MEET

The Rise of the Black Student Union
at Berea College in Kentucky
1968-1970
A Memoir

Edward D. Smith

Foreword by Claudette Schmidt Smith

All Black Students Meet: The Rise of the Black Student Union at Berea College, in Kentucky, 1968-1970

Cover: Photograph is from an article entitled "Black Students at Berea Occupy President's Office to Protest Arrests and to Express Other Grievances," March 1970. Article with photograph appeared in The Berea Alumnus May-June, 1970. Courtesy Claudette Schmidt's Personal Scrapbook, 1968-72.

Frontispiece: Members of the Black Student Union as photographed in the Alumni Building Lounge, Fall 1970. The photograph is from the Berea College Yearbook, 1971 (volume is not online), p. 176, which was the first time the BSU appeared in the Berea Chimes. From original volume, courtesy Claudette Schmidt's Personal Collection.

The title, "All Black Students Meet," is based upon the four words that Kenneth Miller boldly posted on the Alumni Building bulletin board. His action led to the initial meeting and formal organization of the BSU.

Dedicated to Ann Beard and Ken Miller, for starting it all!

Contents

Foreword

"All Black Students Meet," a memoir by Edward D. Smith, is a fascinating account of the very beginnings of the Black Student Union on the Berea College campus in Kentucky. The story begins during the racially turbulent Spring Semester of 1968 and ends with the BSU as a firmly established cultural organization at the close of the Fall Semester of 1970.

Edward entered Berea in the Fall of 1967 and graduated in December 1970. So he witnessed the creation and growth of the BSU during those first two crucial years, 1968-1970. As a keen observer of human events, Edward is aptly able to tell this fascinating story. He personally knew the key persons involved in the initial decision to call for "all black students [to] meet," and he later served as an elected officer during this critical two-year period. Therefore, he has attempted to tell the whole story, including the internal politics and disagreements within the organization.

From the opening chapter which places the story within the context of the Civil Rights Movement and emerging Black Power Movement, to the book's Epilogue which recounts the BSU's amazing accomplishments, and lasting legacy; Edward has woven a narrative that is scholarly written, sometimes funny from our 21st century point of view, but always dramatically told. After reading this story, one might conclude that although much progress has been made in race relations, much work is yet to be done, as seen by the recent revival of black student activism in the "Black Lives Matter" movement on campuses around the country.

In addition to the many photographs and documents contained in the seven chapters of this memoir, the book also includes eleven appendices (Appendix A-K) that further enlivens and illustrates the work. Some of the photographs and documents in the appendices illustrate Edward's involvement in other college-related activities and events of the period.

As Edward's dear friend at Berea from the Fall of 1968 through his graduation in December 1970, and now his wife of 42 years,

I know that Berea has influenced him greatly throughout his life. I have assisted him in searching our files for Berea related documents, and I have watched him work late into the night, so I know that this project has been very important to him. So I want to congratulate him on its completion. The book is a good read, and I recommend it to everyone who might be interested in the history of black student activism, and especially the rise of BSUs in the late 1960s. As a fellow Berea graduate, I also highly recommend the book to all Bereans.

Claudette Schmidt Smith
Berea Class of 1972

Preface

Controversy has surrounded the birth of the Berea College Black Student Union (BSU) since its inception in the Spring of 1968.

This book will attempt to give a history of the organization's earliest beginnings, and answer some of the questions that arose at the time, and that are probably being asked about until this day.

As a student who attended the first meeting, I wish to record my personal recollections while they are still fresh on my mind at ages 65-67. I was 18 years of age at the time the BSU was founded, so those events occurred during a very formative period of my life. Hence, those events have influenced my life work, especially my career path, first as a government historian and later as a government archivist.

This narrative is based on my personal memories of events and conversations from the earliest years of the BSU, 1968-70; and upon some important BSU related documents (like the BSU Constitution, the Negro Studies Committee Reports, and black cultural programs) that my wife and I have preserved over the years.

Throughout this narrative, I have quoted from memory, some of statements and conversations of other observers and participants. I am fully aware that the personal memories of others may differ from mine. In several specific instances where I am aware of differences in memories, I have explained them in footnotes. I can only hope that the recollections of others do not differ greatly from mine.

To date, there has been no detailed account written of the early years of this organization. So it is more than fitting and proper that I record my memories, and display some of the documents and photographs from those early years.

Acknowledgments

I am extremely grateful to my wife, Claudette Schmidt Smith, who came to Berea a year after my arrival. During her four years at the college, she meticulously put together a scrapbook that contains some very important articles and programs relating to the BSU during those early years. Her scrapbook has been an invaluable source of information and has aided in refreshing my memories of those formative years.

I also want to thank Ms. Rachel Vagts, Head of Special Collections and Archives at Berea College, for allowing me to freely use copies of photographs from the "Berea College Digital Collections." These photographs not only helped to refresh my memories of the period, but they also have richly illustrated this book.

My acknowledgments also go out to former Berea student Mike Clark, and Lexington Herald-Leader newspaper reporter, Tom Eblens, for allowing me to use the 1965 photograph of Berea students in Montgomery, Alabama. Mike took the original picture, and the online copy I have used is from Tom's February 12, 2015, blog in the newspaper.

My thanks also go out to Julius Lester, university professor, social critic, and author of Look Out Whitey and many other books. When contacted he did not hesitate to allow me to use his online photograph.

I also want to thank Dr. Genevieve Skaker, Associate Dean, Indiana University School of Liberal Arts at Indiana University-Purdue University Indianapolis (IUPUI), and Mr. Gregory H. Mobley, Archives Specialist, IUPUI University Library and Special Collections and Archives. Together they granted me permission to use the online photograph of the late Dr. Joseph Taylor.

I also want to thank Professor Andrew Baskin, of Berea College for directing me to Sharyn Mitchell, Research Services Specialist, Special Collections & Archives at Berea College. I especially thank Sharyn and her student worker, for finding the signature page for a November 26, 1967 petition by 18 black students in support of a "Negro History" course. The document (with commentary) appears in Appendix K).

Finally, I want to acknowledge all of the students, who came together to form the BSU in the Spring of 1968, and also those students who arrived during the following crucial two years. All of you (despite differences in opinions) helped establish an ongoing and lasting legacy of "black culture" at Berea College, which was, in fact, the primary objective spelled out in the BSU Constitution from the very beginning. For this lasting cultural achievement, we can all be proud!

I

Historical Context:
Berea Student Involvement in the Civil Rights Movement, 1965

The birth of the Berea College BSU should be seen within the broader context of the national civil rights movement of the 1950s and 1960s. By the end of 1965, the major battles against legal segregation had been won. Many of the foot soldiers of those battles had been college students, black and white, who had marched together under the umbrella organization known as the Student Nonviolent Coordinating Committee (SNCC).

Although there was no official SNCC organization on Berea's campus, a contingent of Berea College Students (white and black), along with some faculty, participated in the Selma to Montgomery Voting Rights Marches in March 1965.[1] After my arrival at Berea, I had the pleasure of becoming acquainted with at least three of the black students who had participated in the Montgomery March of March 25, 1965: Ann Beard (Grundy), Jerry Harris, and Sarah Wade (Brown).[2] Ann Beard, in particular, would remain politically active on campus, and in the Spring of 1968, would be instrumental in organizing the BSU.

---

[1]The college administration, faculty and student body were divided over the issue of the group's participation in the March. Among the Faculty attending the March were: Dr. Donald Graham, Dr. Richard Drake, and Dr. Thomas Kreider. For Dr. Graham's and Dr. Drake's stories of the March, see Berea Carter G. Woodson Center, Video & Publications Library, "Selma-Montgomery 50th Year Celebration Reception in the Carter G. Woodson Center;" at https://www.berea.edu/cgwc/video-library.

[2]Nomamdi Ellis, "Walking in the Footsteps of Peace: Forty Years of Civil Rights Marching." Berea, Kentucky: Berea College Magazine, Volume 75 (Spring 2005), pp. 16-24. Ann and Sarah were interviewed for this article; see online at: https://www.berea.edu/magazine/files/2014/11/75.4-2005-Spring2.pdf. See also, Dwayne Mack, "'Ain't Gonna Let Nobody Turn Me Around': Berea College's Participation in the Selma to Montgomery March." Cincinnati & Louisville: Ohio Valley History, Volume 5 (Spring 2005), pp. 43-62. All three participants, Ann, Jerry and Sarah were interviewed for Dwayne Mack's article; see online at: http://library.cincymuseum.org/journals/files/ovh/v05/n3/ovh-v05-n3-ain-043.pdf

From left to right, Ann Beard, Jerry Harris, and Sarah Wade, (shown here in their senior class photographs), were three of the Berea black students who had marched in Montgomery, Alabama in 1965.[3]

Fifty-eight Berea students and faculty members joined the Selma to Montgomery March outside Montgomery in 1965. Ann Beard is wearing the light colored hat on the left holding the Berea banner. Jerry Harris is in the center behind the banner in the dark dress coat and tie. The man in the light sports coat with his back to the camera, is probably Dr. Thomas Kreider, one of the faculty members who accompanied the students. The photograph was taken by one of the Berea College students, Mike Clark.[4]

---

[3]Photographs courtesy The Berea College Digital Collections, The Berea Yearbooks Online (hereafter referred to as Berea Chimes Online), 1968, pp. 22, 41 and 1969, p.60.
[4]Photograph and partial caption taken from Tom Eblen's Blog entitled "50 years later, Berea alumni say Selma march changed their lives," Lexington Herald-Leader, February 15, 2015; see online at: http://tomeblen.bloginky.com/2015/02/15/50-years-later-berea-alumni-say-selma-march-changed-their-lives/

Emergence of the Black Power Movement, 1966

Gradually black students nationally in SNCC, and on college campuses in general, grew disenchanted with the continued resistance and violence displayed by some southern whites who continued to oppose the efforts of blacks to register to vote. So in June 1966, the new chairman of SNCC, Stokely Carmichael, declared that Negroes or colored people (the terminology of that period), should think in terms of "Black Power" instead of seeking white support.[5]

Carmichael's coinage of the phrase "Black Power" in the summer of 1966, was viewed by the news media as radical and cutting-edge, so the words became popular. Black students were to be taught that "Black Is Beautiful." They were to be taught to strive to achieve a political "black consciousness," and become informed of their history and common problems. This would lead to group solidarity and the election of black office holders, and the attainment of black economic power.[6]

A few months prior to the advent of the Black Power Movement, however, a group interested in raising the "black consciousness" of students on a predominantly white campus, organized the first "Black Student Union" in the nation in March 1966, at San Francisco State University. The name "Black Student Union" caught on, and similarly named organizations soon appeared on campuses in Oregon and Washington State. The name was later adopted by organizations appearing in Utah, Kansas, and Kentucky (probably first at the University of Louisville), and then around the nation.[7]

---

[5]John Hope Franklin, From Slavery to Freedom: A History of Negro Americans. 5th Edition, New York: Alfred A Knopf, 1980, pp. 481-482.

[6]James A. Banks, and Cherry A. Banks. March Toward Freedom: A History of Black Americans. Belmont, California: Lear Siegler, Inc./Fearon Publishers, 1974, p.138.

[7]Ibram H. Rogers. The Black Campus Movement: Black Students and the Racial Reconstruction of Higher Education, 1965-1972. New York: Palgrave Macmillan, 2012, or online at: https://books.google.com/books?id=3ZxiAQAAQBAJ&pg=PR139&lpg=PR139&dq=Tricia+Navara&-source=bl&ots=q6is0DxCbk&sig=3JDsiyyKHrsVVyOnqsHT4819hcs&hl=en&sa=X&ved=0a-hUKEwjT5q3OxPrOAhWEqh4KHRikCi8Q6AEIlzAB#v=onepage&q=Tricia%20Navara&f=-false. Dr. J. Blaine Hudson, who entered the University of Louisville as a student in 1967 and became a BSU organizer, has said that the Louisville BSU was organized in 1968, and that the King Assassination in April 1968 was the real catalyst that started BSU activism at Louisville. See and listen to his interview online at: KET Education, Living the Story: The Civil Rights Movement in Kentucky. https://www.ket.org/education/resources/living-sto-ry-civil-rights-movement-kentucky/

II

A Winning Bet:
The Formation of the Berea BSU,
Spring Semester 1968

As indicated earlier, the first Black Student Union in the nation is said to have been started at San Francisco State University in March 1966.[8] The Berea College BSU was formed two years later. The year 1968 was a fertile time for the creation of BSUs around the nation on predominately white campuses, especially in the aftermath of the assassination of Dr. Martin Luther King. It is my recollection, that the BSU at the University of Louisville, predated the organization at Berea. After the BSU was formed at Berea, the President of the BSU at the University of Louisville was invited to Berea to give advice and support.[9]

According to the unofficial history of the San Francisco State University BSU, that organization was started with a bet. The "bet was that" a "black student movement" could not be built "on a predominately white campus." Apparently, one black student accepted the bet.[10]

The Berea College BSU, according to my recollections, was also started with a bet. The idea of starting a black student organization on campus originated with a small group of activist black seniors, that included Ann Beard and a young man from Louisville named Kenneth Miller.[11] They often hung out in the Alumni Building Snack Bar and talked about the issues of the day. They were sometimes joined by a young white professor (the college had no black professors at that

---

[8]Sam Whiting, "The Black Student Union at SFSU started it all," San Francisco Chronicle, February 1, 2010, at: http://www.sfgate.com/news/article/The-Black-Student-Union-at-SFSU-started-it-all-3274175.php. See also Ibram S. Rogers, The Black Campus Movement: Black Students and the Radical Reconstruction of Higher Education, 1965-1972, New York: Palgrave Macmillan, 2012, or online at: https://books.google.com/books?id=3ZxiAQAAQBAJ&pg=PR139&lpg=PR139&d-q=Tricia+Navara&source=bl&ots=q6is0DxCbk&sig=3JDsiyyKHrsVVyOn-qsHT4819hcs&hl=en&sa=X&ved=0ahUKEwjT5q3OxPrOAhWEqh4KHRikCi8Q6A-EIIzAB#v=onepage&q=Tricia%20Navara&f=false
[9]The President of the University of Louisville BSU was invited to address the newly formed Berea BSU during the Fall 1968-Spring 1969 school year under the Presidency of Odell Smith.
[10]Whiting, "The Black Student Union at SFSU started it all," San Francisco Chronicle, February 1, 2010.
[11]Among the other activist black seniors that I sometimes saw gathered with Ann at one of the front tables in the Snack Bar were: Ann's friend Gwen Hale (Daugherty), Barbara Durr (Fleming), Frieda Hopkins (Outlaw), and Sarah Wade (Brown).

time) from the Department of Philosophy and Religion, Dr. Donald Graham, who had marched with some of the students in Montgomery.

My recollections are that while involved in a discussion about what black student organizations were doing on other predominantly white campuses, the black students indicated to Dr. Graham that they intended to start an organization at Berea. They felt that they needed a distinct organization that would address the social-cultural needs of the black students, and that would also challenge the seeming hypocrisy of the college with its all-white faculty and its failure to fully acknowledge its Afro-American past. Dr. Graham, probably in disbelief, bet or warned (apparently no money was involved) that if anyone dared ask all black students at Berea to meet, "all hell" would break loose. Ken Miller, who was very talkative and charismatic, already had his mind made up. He posted a sign on the bulletin board in the Alumni Building simply saying **"All Black Students Meet."** Shortly afterward, "all hell" did break lose.[12]

Ann Beard and Kenneth Miller started it all![13]

There were immediate demands from some faculty and administrators that the sign should be removed because the use of the word "black" was offensive. There was also general wonderment about why on earth "Negro" students at a college with an interracial history like Berea, want to meet separately? The sign was taken

[12]While visiting Dr. Graham's gift shop in Berea in the year 2006, I asked him if he remembered the incident. He said he did not recall the incident, or Miller. As we talked on for a while, however, he snapped his finger and begin to smile, and said "Oh yea, now it coming back to me." He said that he had begun to remember Ken, if not the specific incident.

[13]Photographs courtesy The Berea College Digital Collections, Berea Chimes Online, 1966, p.147; 1968, p. 59.

down, but Ken Miller immediately put up another one, which was allowed to remain.[14]

The necessity of the proposed meeting was also questioned by some black students, who were confused about its purpose, and also rather embarrassed and offended by the use of the word "black." I remember walking to the initial BSU meeting with another black student, who said that he was going to the meeting, but "they better not call me black!"[15]

The Initial Meeting

The initial meeting that had caused so much anxiety was held in the Alumni Building, with Ken Miller, presiding. Despite the anxiety it had created, the meeting was well attended. In 1968, there were only about 57 black students at Berea,[16] and I would estimate that at least 20-25 attended the initial meeting. Ken was quite a firebrand, so he was able to press home the importance of the meeting. Those in attendance at the initial meeting quickly agreed that there were lots of complaints to level against the college. I remember at least ten major complaints. Among the complaints were the following:

- the lack of discussions about race in chapel and convocations;
- the dearth of black chapel and convocation speakers;

---

[14]Ann Beard's recollections of these initial events are slightly different from mine, and she was directly involved, while I was only an observer and listener. Ann, for example, does not mention Dr. Donald Graham's warning. Ann says that Ken Miller's initial sign said "All blacks," and that the Dean of Women, Ann Marshall, ripped the sign down. So Ken Miller's second sign, according to Ann, was in coded language: "All ye who use Peach and Glo, Royal Crown Hair Grease—and he went through all of this stuff, you know--Press and Comb, please meet in the Ballard Room. At 6:30 we were all there, every black student on the planet." See Ann Beard Grundy's oral history contribution to Catherine Fosl's and Tracy E. K'Meyer's edition of Freedom on the Border: An Oral History of the Civil Rights Movement in Kentucky (Lexington, Kentucky: The University of Kentucky Press, 2009), p. 195, and online at: https://books.google.com/books?id=bnj0JHhoZ4oC&lpg=PT228&ots=VWgsOiikh&dq=berea%20college%20bsu&pg=PT228#v=twopage&q=berea%20college%20bsu&f=true

[15]My friend (Homer Williams) who accompanied me to the initial meeting knew from experience, how the word "black" had been used to embarrass, humiliate and dehumanize. Only recently his white roommate had flown into a rage, and called him a "black bastard;" thereby forcing him to move out and find a more enlightened white roommate.

[16]Not counting the 6 black students from the African continent.

- the total absence of black faculty;

- the paltry number of black students;

- the absence of black related courses in the curriculum;

- subtle racist attitudes showed by well-meaning officials and faculty;

- prejudiced white students who refused to room with black students;[17]

- dorm mothers who frowned upon interracial dating;[18]

- and the infamous annual "Star Lite Hike," which generally excluded about half of the black freshmen women, since there were not enough black males to go around.[19]

There also was one more quietly voiced complaint. The new college President (Dr. Willis Weatherford), was very well-liked, but he found it rather difficult to transition from using the once polite southern term "Niggra" in his speeches. To black students, "Negro" was the accepted terminology of the day, while "Niggra" was seen as an outdated "slavery-time" racist word. The President's continued use of this antiquated terminology especially irritated many of the black female students. Although he did eventually make the transition to simply using the word "black," many students felt that it took him much too long to adapt.

Election of the first President

Wallace Gatewood, a college senior, was elected the first BSU President at its initial meeting. Gatewood was a very good speaker, with a very good vocabulary. He also was well-liked by everyone. Perhaps the only critique ever made of him was that he studied his dictionary, and daily practiced his vocabulary on other students,

---

[17]There were reports of white female students who had refused to unpack, until they were relieved from rooming with black female students.

[18]Reportedly, the dorm director of Kentucky Hall had recently notified the parents of a white female student that their daughter was dating a black male student. She apparently thought the parents ought to know because they might not approve of interracial dating.

[19]The Star Lite Hike was a "blind date" in which the dorm Junior Assistants (JA's) matched up freshmen males and females at the very beginning of the school year for a romantic group hike at sundown. In 1967 there were eleven black freshman females and only five black males; and there was no interracial pairing.

which was actually a compliment![20] I believe all, or at least most of the four other elected officers (not counting the Faculty Sponsor), were seniors. They were viewed as the natural leaders due to their maturity, although we all knew that they would be graduating within a few of months, and leaving us to carry on the struggle.

Wallace Gatewood, first President of the BSU.[21]

Selection of the first Faculty Sponsor

Every student organization on campus was required to have a Faculty Sponsor. There were no black faculty persons, so the black students immediately agreed at their initial meeting to ask Dr. James Y. Holloway if he would serve as the sponsor. Dr. Holloway, Professor of Philosophy and Religion, was a natural choice since he was known to be a vocal supporter of the national civil rights movement. He was a member, along with Dr. Martin Luther King Jr., of the interracial organization known as the Council of Southern Churchmen. Dr. Holloway agreed to serve as the first BSU Sponsor, but only in an "advisory" capacity. He never wanted it to be said that he was "running the BSU." I recall that he was invited to, and attended only one meeting

---

[20]A female friend once remarked that she often felt the need of a dictionary in order to follow Gatewood's causal conversations.
[21]Photograph courtesy The Berea College Digital Collections, Berea Chimes Online, 1968, p. 29.

Dr. James Holloway, first Faculty Sponsor of the BSU[22]

The Creation of a Myth

It was perhaps due to the fact that the BSU at its initial meeting, agreed to ask Dr. Holloway to serve as its first Faculty Sponsor, that a myth developed that the organization was started by white people. There is no truth in this myth.

As I have stated earlier, the formation of the BSU was initiated by black students Ann Beard, Ken Miller, and a few other seniors who often discussed issues among themselves in the Alumni Building Snack Bar. They were aware that BSU organizations were being formed at other predominantly white schools, so they came up with the idea of establishing a BSU at Berea.

I have also already stated, that according to my recollections, Dr. Donald Graham, a young white faculty member who had marched in Montgomery, Alabama, and sometimes joined the black students in the Snack Bar, bet or warned (probably in disbelief), that a call for all black students to meet would cause "all hell" to break loose. The original idea, however, was not Dr. Graham's; rather it was Ann Beard's and a few other black seniors, chief among them being Ken Miller.

The myth has had a long existence. It was probably generated by black students, who at the time, were afraid and confused about the purpose of the organization. I heard the myth stated explicitly for the first time in the Fall of 1970 by a black student who had entered Berea in 1969. Later on, in the 1980s, long

[22]Photograph courtesy The Berea College Digital Collections, Berea Chimes Online, 1966, p. 137.

after I had left Berea, a young woman working in Washington, D.C., who had graduated from Berea in the late 1970s, asked me if it was true that whites had started the organization? My answer to her was an emphatic no! It is my hope that the details outlined above in this memoir will forever bury the myth.

The BSU Constitution

One of the first questions the new organization had to ask itself was what kind of an organization was it going to be? So the BSU set about drafting a constitution. The constitution clearly stated that the primary goals of the BSU were cultural in nature. The four objects of the new organization were:

1. To increase the knowledge of Black Culture.

2. To stimulate interest in Black Culture on the Berea campus.

3. To promote the cultural enrichment of the Black community.

4. To better Black-White relations.

The black students were well aware of the college's long-standing commitment to interracial education. So the new organization had no desire to segregate itself on a predominately white campus. Therefore, Article 3 of the BSU constitution clearly stated that:

"Any student of Berea College who shows a sincere interest in our objectives is eligible for membership."

The organization would attempt to support itself financially by accessing membership dues of $1.00 per semester. The six elected officers were to be: the President, Vice President, Secretary, Financial Chairman, Reporter, and Faculty Sponsor. The organization would meet at least twice per month.

Page 1 of a notice to black students (ca. Spring-Fall, 1968), of an upcoming important meeting. Included with the notice was a draft copy of the BSU Constitution.[23]

[23]Courtesy Edward Smith's Personal Collection.

The Black Students Union will meet on Sunday Afternoon at 6:00 P.M. in the Taylor Room. Please come. This meeting is very Important! There will be discussion on the organization itself and membership. Please bring your dues for this semester which is $1.00. This fee is to be paid Sunday if you intend to be a member of the Black Students Union.

Thank-you

Page 2 of notice to black students (ca. Spring-Fall, 1968), of an upcoming important meeting. Included with the notice was a draft copy of the BSU Constitution.[24]

[24]Courtesy Edward Smith's Personal Collection.

Article I.   Name: BLACK STUDENT UNION
              The name of this organization shall be:

Article II.   Object
              The objects of this organization shall be:
              1. To increase the knowledge of the Black culture.
              2. To stimulate interest in the Black culture on the Berea
                  College campus.
              3. To promote cultural enrichment of the Black community.
              4. *To keep Black unity vital*

Article III. Membership
              Section I. Any student of Berea College who shows a sincere
                  interest in our objectives is eligible for membership.

Article IV.   Dues
              Section I. The organization will be financially supported by
                  dues from members of the organization.
                  $1 per semester

Article V.   Officers
              Section I. The officers shall be: president, vice-president,
                  secretary, financial chairman, reporter, sponsor.
                  Each officer shall be elected to serve for a term of one
                  year with exception of the sponsor.

Article VI.   Duties of Officers

              Section I. It shall be the duty of the president to preside at
                  all meetings. He shall be a member ex-officio of all
                  committees. He shall call special meetings and perform
                  all other duties usually incident ot the office.

              Section II. It shall be the duty of the vice president to assist
                  the president and preside in his absence.

              Section III. It shall be the duty of the secretary to keep a
                  written record of all meetings and complete record of
                  membership.

              Section IV. It shall be the duty of the financial chairman to
                  collect contributions; to keep records of all money of thee
                  organization; and to pay out money only upon order signed
                  by the president.

              Section V. It shall be the duty of the reporter to keep events of the
                  organization adequately publicized.

Page 1 of the BSU Constitution (ca. Spring-Fall, 1968).[25]

---

[25]Courtesy Edward Smith's Personal Collection.

Article VII. Meetings
      Section I. The club shall meet at least twice a month with
         possibilities of special call meetings subject at anytime.

      Section II. The recommended order of business at regular meetings
         shall be as follows:
         Call to order by the president
         Reading of the minutes
         Reports of committees
         Proposals for members
         General business
         Program
         Adjournment

Article VIII. Committees
      Section I. The president shall appoint all standing committees
         chairmen.

Article IX. Amendments
      This constitution may be amended by a two-thirds vote of the
      attending majority and approval of the cabinet or general faculty.

Article X. By-laws
      Such by-laws are necessary to perpetuate the growth and development
      of the organization in harmony with the spirit and purpose of this
      constitution may be adopted by the club at any time.

Page 2 of the BSU Constitution (ca. Spring-Fall, 1968).[26]

[26]Courtesy Edward Smith's Personal Collection.

Growth of Black Consciousness

The most immediate effect of the formation of the BSU was the rapid rise of an atmosphere of political and cultural "black consciousness" on campus. Prior to the formation of the BSU, there was little "black consciousness" on campus. This was before the age of the "Afro" hairstyle. Only one lone black female student, Gwendolyn Hale (Daugherty), a politically active senior, proudly wore a "Natural" hairstyle on campus. Many blacks would not even smile, "nod," or speak, as they approached and passed each other on campus. It was common to see one lone black student tagging along behind 5 or 6 whites, or simply walking alone. The campus atmosphere was as if there was an unspoken rule that the small number of blacks (57 in all) were to blend in with the white students as individuals, and remain as low key and as invisible as possible. There was, of course, a small number of black males (maybe a half dozen) who lived on Dana 3, and prided themselves on going to Richmond on the weekends, partying, fraternizing with as many women as possible, and referring to blacks on campus as "spelbs." They were seen as small-town boys trying to exhibit street smarts. They exhibited no black political consciousness, and no one took these guys seriously. All of this began to change after the formation of the BSU in the Spring of 1968.

Gwen Hale[27]

---

[27]Photograph courtesy The Berea Digital Collections, Berea Chimes Online, 1968, p. 29. Gwen Hale and Ann Beard were two of the most politically active students (black or white) on campus. They had been among the first group of Berea College anti-poverty Appalachian Volunteers in 1965, and remained politically active through their graduation in June 1968. See Msiba Ann Beard Grundy interviewed by Margaret Brown, Louie B. Nunn Center for Oral History, University of Kentucky Libraries, Appalachia Oral History Collection, War On Poverty Oral History Project, June 5, 1991. Listen online at https://nyx.uky.edu/oh/render.php?cachefile=1991oh187_app312_grundy_ohm.xml

The Beginnings of the Black Ensemble

One of the first things some of the black female students decided to do, was to gather together "to sang the kinds of songs we are used to singing." This idea was first suggested by freshman student Eva Reed (Ovuworie) in the Spring of 1968, and the idea caught on. The first gathering was held just inside the Alumni Building's front entrance, in the first private room on the right. This room had a piano, and freshman student Gay Nell Bell (Duckett) was the first pianist.

Most black students were familiar with gospel music and enjoyed singing it, although, in 1968, some more formal black churches still frowned on it. I recall that a freshman female student, Susan Smith (Grant), who served with me on the Negro Studies Committee,[28] asked me if my home church allowed us to sing like that. I told her, yes, they allowed our "junior choir" (teenage choir) to sing like that, but that the "senior choir" (adult choir) still only sang hymns and anthems. Susan replied that the young people at her church also wanted to sing gospel, but the adults would not allow them to do so.

The informal singing group which Eva Reed started in the Spring of 1968, continued to sing unofficially in the private room in the Alumni Building, and in the female dorm rooms throughout 1968 and into 1969, until the arrival of the first black Counselor, Mr. Melvin Marshall, in the Fall of 1969. Shortly after his arrival at Berea, Mr. Marshall and a student, Charles Crowe, formally organized the Black Ensemble, now known as the Black Music Ensemble.

Eva Reed[29]   Gay Nell Bell[30]

---

[28]Susan and I also worked together on the College Food Service Line our freshman year, along with Eva Reed.
[29]Photograph courtesy The Berea College Digital Collections, Berea Chimes Online, 1970, p. 55.
[30]Photograph courtesy The Berea College Digital Collections, Berea Chimes Online, 1969, p. 92.

The Work of the Negro Studies Committee

Before outgoing BSU President, Wallace Gatewood graduated in the Spring of 1968, he along with senior student Ann Beard, asked two freshmen students, Susan Smith and myself, if we would replace them on the Berea College Negro Studies Committee, which had been appointed by President Weatherford on February 14, 1968. This indicates that the BSU was no doubt organized after the appointment of the Negro Studies Committee, thus the name "Negro Studies," rather than "Black Studies;" the latter terminology was not yet in vogue at Berea.[31] Susan and I agreed to serve on the committee, so President Weatherford officially appointed us on May 4, 1968, and we attended the last two meetings along with Wallace and Ann in order to familiarize ourselves with the work of the Committee.

---

[31]When I entered Berea in the Fall of 1967, the use of the term "black" was still frowned upon by many African Americans and whites.

REPORT OF THE NEGRO STUDIES COMMITTEE

Part One: Membership and Activity

I. Membership

The Negro Studies Committee was appointed February 14, 1968 by President Willis D. Weatherford, Jr. He and Dean Louis Smith were ex officio members but met with the Committee only at the beginning. Other members appointed at that time were:

Faculty members: Matilda Cartledge
James Holloway
Emily Ann Smith
James Stermer
John White
Robert Menefee, Chairman

Student members: Ann Beard
Wallace Gatewood

Recognizing that its work would not be completed by June, the Committee asked that student membership be given continuity by the addition of two students who would not be graduating. On May 4, 1968, President Weatherford appointed the following students who attended the last two meetings of the Committee in May:

Susan Smith
Edward D. Smith

II. Meetings

The first meeting of the Negro Studies Committee was held February 22 with President Weatherford and Dean Smith. During the twelve working weeks remaining in the spring semester, the Committee held eleven meetings. Attendance usually numbered 6-8 members, and fell below 5 members on only one occasion. Meetings began at 4:30 and continued past 6:00 in nearly every case — one did not adjourn until almost 7:00.

The number and duration of meetings (especially during the spring semester) give some indication of the concern which members of the Negro Studies Committee brought to their work and of the effort devoted to it. Going beyond this, however, it should be noted that the discussions involved very wide philosophical differences and the deepest personal feelings of the members of the Committee. Under these circumstances, it would not have been surprising if the Committee had politely avoided the really tough issues and dealt only with superficial aspects, or, on the other hand, if the deep and intense differences had brought the Committee's work to a standstill and made significant conclusions impossible. That neither of these occurred is something of which the Committee members are, quite frankly, proud. Though every meeting of the Committee was strenuous, sometimes even painful, no one ceased to listen, to learn, and to participate.

III. Topics Considered

In a general way the subjects to which the Committee addressed itself may be

Page 1 of the Report of the Negro Studies Committee, Fall 1968, showing the names of the Committee members.[32]

The faculty members comprising the Negro Studies Committee were: Dr. James Holloway, Dr. James Stermer, Dr. Robert Menefee, Professor Emily Ann Smith, Dr. Matilda Cartledge, and Dr. John White. President Weatherford and Dean Louis Smith were ex officio members.

---

[32]Courtesy Edward Smith's Personal Collection. For the full report, see Appendix A.

A composite of "The Negro Studies Committee," established in February 1968. Top row: Dr. James Holloway, Dr. James Stermer, Dr. Robert Menefee, Professor Emily Ann Smith. Middle row: Dr. Matilda Cartledge, Dr. John White, student members Ann Beard, and Wallace Gatewood. Bottom row: Susan Smith and Edward Smith were appointed to replace Ann and Wallace in May 1968.[33]

This committee's objective was to come up with ways to integrate the study of the black experience not only into the curriculum, but also into the life of the campus community, through speakers at chapel services, convocations, and cultural events. My most memorable meeting occurred when the Committee invited Dr. Carol

[33]Photographs courtesy The Berea College Digital Collections, Berea Chimes Online, 1965, pp. 105, 109; 1966, pp. 131, 137-138, 149; 1967, p. 44; 1969, pp. 99-100; 1970, p. 82.

Gesner to discuss chapel services, convocations, and other cultural events on campus. Although Dr. Gesner was not a member of the Committee, she had a decidedly strong point of view on the subject. So there emerged two sharply divided points of view at that meeting.

Dr. Carol Gesner[34]

On the one hand, Dr. Gesner argued ably that "we ought to cool it" on having speakers come to talk about race relations. She felt that we had had "enough for a while," and that we could address interracial education in cultural and less confrontational ways. She later would be instrumental in bringing the "Panamanian Dancers" (a dance group of color) to Berea to perform.

On the other hand, Dr. Jim Holloway argued just as ably for bringing more speakers to discuss the issue of race. Dr. Holloway asked Dr. Gesner: "How can we cool it Carol when our cities are burning?" He would later bring the black activist, writer, and scholar, Julius Lester, author of the book Look Out Whitey, into his home in Berea to speak to interested students.

Julius Lester[35]

---

[34]Photograph courtesy The Berea College Digital Collections, Berea Chimes Online, 1966, p. 131
[35]Photograph online at http://www.teachingbooks.net/ tb.cgi?aid=1596&s=i&a=1&a2=1. Courtesy Julius Lester.

The initial "Report of the Negro Studies Committee" which was issued on September 23, 1968, came down somewhere in the middle of these two points of view. The Committee agreed that: "As a nation, as Christians, as a college, we face a crisis." The crisis, however, had arisen "not from rioting and violence" (as Dr. Holloway had suggested), "but from the fact that God [has] made of one blood, and man has divided." The report went on to state emphatically that: "Whatever Berea is now doing in this regard is surely not sufficient for the time and the place." On the issue of chapel and convocation speakers, the Report recommended that: "The Sunday night chapel services should include: Worship services led by blacks as well as by whites." The college should also invite: "Speakers who might help us think more deeply concerning the Christian commitment to brotherhood."[36]

---

[36]Quoted from the Report of the Negro Studies Committee, Fall 1968, p. 3. For the full report, see Appendix A.

III

Speaking Out:
Campus-wide Political Awakening,
Late Spring 1968

The late Spring of 1968, were exciting times at Berea, although this period would also witness two national tragedies. These were exciting times at Berea, however, because heated political discussions would occasionally erupt in the Alumni Building Lobby or in the Alumni Building Lounge. I am not even sure if the gatherings were well planned in advance. Tensions over the Vietnam War were beginning to be voiced at Berea, and discussions of race relations, the Vietnam War, and the War on Poverty, were often intertwined. Some who were involved in these discussions were no doubt aware of the fact that, Dr. King, had given a speech at Riverside Church in New York on April 4, 1967, in which he had come out against the Vietnam War, and that he also had planned a Poor People's Campaign for Jobs and Justice for the Summer of 1968.

One evening, for example, in the late Spring of 1968, a liberal group of Berea College "anti-poverty" Appalachian Volunteers (all white males) set up tables in the Alumni Building Lobby about dinner time, and begin handing out literature. A group of physically big ultra-conservative white male students became angry and ordered the Appalachian Volunteers to get "that trash off of the campus." The Appalachian Volunteers were physically just as large, so both sides agreed to discuss their views like educated people, and although they never agreed, the discussion went well into the evening.

On another occasion, in the late Spring of 1968, a discussion on race seem to have erupted out of nowhere in the Alumni Building Lounge, although it may have been planned, because some faculty members were present. It appeared to me at the time, however, that as students finished dinner, some simply drifted into the Lounge to relax and watch television, but suddenly found themselves in the middle of a spirited discussion. At one point in the discussion, my sister, Evelyn Juanita Smith (Lee) who was a senior, but never attended BSU meetings, and was not considered politically active in any way, responded quickly to a general inquiry about racial prejudice among the faculty. She said that a particular Nursing Faculty member had gathered the black nursing students and lectured them on why they were going to have a "hard time." The Nursing Faculty person said that she knew this to be true because she had not only taught black students, but she had also been a student with them, and "they just tended not to do very well." So she warned the black nursing students, that "they would have to work real hard." A faculty member (Dr. Donald Graham), who was present at this Alumni Building discussion, along with several black students who were also present, expressed their surprise that Juanita had spoken out so forcefully that evening. At another point in this discussion, the always fiery Ken Miller, pointed out to a fellow white student, the difference in their racial histories in America. "Your people," Ken snapped, "have enslaved and oppressed my people for years!"

Juanita Smith[37]   Ken Miller[38]

On yet another occasion in the late Spring of 1968, a discussion on race relations that had begun in the Alumni Building Lounge, seemed to have continued into the night outside Dana Dorm. Larry Boulware, a recent Berea graduate (1967), who had briefly returned to campus to visit his brother (senior James "Jim" Boulware), was invited by BSU President Wallace Gatewood, to give an impromptu address to the students. Larry and Jim had once played basketball for Berea, and both were physics and pre-med majors. After graduating from Berea, Larry had gone on to do pre-medical studies at Haverford College near Philadelphia. In addressing the Berea students that evening, Larry reportedly expressed regret for his lack of involvement in student activism while enrolled at Berea. He indicated that his transformation had occurred during the Philadelphia Student Riots in the Fall of 1967 when he began to feel

[37]Photograph courtesy The Berea College Digital Collections, Berea Chimes Online, 1964, p. 76.
[38]Photograph courtesy The Berea College Digital Collections, Berea Chimes Online, 1964, p. 72.

that he should have been out throwing bricks with his fellow young blacks, rather than studying inside the safe walls of Haverford College. I worked the dinner shift in Food Service and was unable to attend the address, so later that evening just before dark, I headed over to Dana Dorm to learn what had been said. As I was approaching Dana Hall, I heard tremendously loud voices involved in a heated discussion. As I drew nearer, I could see Larry arguing back and forth with some of the big white Berea basketball players. Larry was physically just as big as these fellows, and smart, so he easily out-argued them in this display of verbal combat. He ended the discussion with some rather salty language reminding the guys that although he had played ball with them and fraternized with them, if they "didn't care about [his] people" then their former camaraderie as players meant nothing to him

Larry Boulware[39]   Jim Boulware[40]

So by the late Spring of 1968, in the male dorms, at least, black students, were beginning to engage white students in open conversations about race, and the antiquated racial beliefs of some of the white guys were being openly exposed. I was sitting around one day in Blue Ridge Hall having a discussion with several white guys when the subject of interracial marriage suddenly came up. The subject came up, perhaps because the U.S. Supreme had only recently declared interracial marriage legal![41] A friendly guy whom I will simply refer to Roy N., immediately said: "Oh no! Nobody should do that because their children will be retarded. Something will be wrong with them." Since I

---

[39]Photograph courtesy The Berea College Digital Collections, Berea Chimes Online, 1967, p. 20

[40]Photograph courtesy The Berea College Digital Collections, Berea Chimes Online, 1967, p. 44

[41]The U. S. Supreme Court declared interracial marriages legal throughout the United State on June 12, 1967. Prior to that time, interracial marriages had been illegal in 16 states, including Kentucky.

had grown up in South Carolina, I was not surprised at his comments, so my response was a simple: "Roy, you don't believe that, do you?" He then replied that: "Everyone knows that if a black and white person produces children, something will be wrong with the children." The other white guys in the room looked rather embarrassed and somewhat uneasy. Suddenly, a white student named Ken Oliver, who served as the JA for the floor, and who just happened to overhear the remarks, stuck his head inside the door and to his great credit spoke up and asked: "Roy where did you get that stupid idea?" Roy became quiet and also began to look embarrassed. I knew that he sincerely believed that he had been correct. He remained friendly, however, and I continued to hope that the discussion that day, had in some measure broadened his view of the human race. After all, Berea's motto at the time was: "God has made of one blood all nations of men." (Acts 17:26).[42]

The MLK Assassination

Dr. Martin Luther King had been invited to speak at Berea the week that he was assassinated (the week of April 4, 1968). He had declined the invitation because of his commitment to Memphis, and the upcoming Poor People's Campaign in Washington. One of the rumors on campus among the black students was that some of the white male students had been heard to say that if King had come to Berea, he "would have gotten it here!"

The evening of King's Assassination is forever etched in my memory. I was alerted by fellow freshman student, Homer Williams, before dinner, that Dr. King had been assassinated in Memphis, and that Dr. James Holloway and a white student named James (Jim) Branscom, were already on their way to Tennessee. Dr. Holloway apparently had contacts in Nashville with ministers close to Dr. King in the interracial organization known as the Council of Southern Churchmen. I was working the dinner shift in the College Food Service, so I went to my job, but the King Assassination was strongly on my mind.

Following dinner, I decided not to follow my normal routine, which would have been to return to my dorm, Blue Ridge. Instead, I lingered in the Alumni Building and begin to look around for some black students to be near. Up until this time, as a freshman student, I had generally avoided going into the Snack Bar. Just the sight of

---

[42]Later changed to: "God has made of one blood all peoples of the earth."

apparently idle students sitting around and looking up to see who came through the open doors, made me nervous. On this occasion, however, I spotted a tiny number of black students (two or three female students), sitting quietly just inside the open doors. So I did something that I had not done up to this time, I went in and sit down in the Snack Bar with that tiny group. I don't think I even said hello, I just sit down. For a while, we all just sit there quietly and said nothing. Then a group of white female students came through the doors, innocently laughing and giggling. All of a sudden, one of the black students, Barbara Durr (Fleming), (I think), said: "Look at them laughing and giggling like nothing has happened." That broke our silence, and I asked if anyone was working on doing something to have the College acknowledge the passing of this great leader? I think it was again, Barbara Durr who told me that Wallace Gatewood was going to gather petitions to present to President Weatherford asking for the cancellation of classes on the day of King's funeral. So off I went immediately to see Gatewood in Dana Dorm. I just felt the need to do something to express my sorrow that evening.

Barbara Durr[43]

Gatewood gave me some petitions and told me that I could gather signatures at my dorm, Blue Ridge, since it was so far removed physically from the rest of the campus. I was anxious to get started, however, so I gathered some signatures before I left Dana, as kind of a trial run. Some white guys signed and some did not. The indecisive expressions on many of their faces are sketched into my memory until this day.

I knew all of the white guys in Blue Ridge by name (there were only three black guys, Charles Crowe, Homer William and myself), so I immediately started going from door to door beginning with the first and

[43]Photograph courtesy The Berea College Digital Library, Berea Chimes Online, 1968, p. 27.

second floors. Most of the guys signed the petition, but some refused. Those who did refuse were generally polite and didn't give a reason for not signing.

When I reached the third floor of Blue Ridge, I pressed forward, although I knew that the guys on this floor were known for their intermural "football" team, and were often a bit rowdy. There was this one over-sized room in particular where about 4 guys lived and other guys "hung out." As I have said, I knew each of these fellows, and they always spoke to me kindly whenever we would pass each other. So without hesitation, I entered the room full of guys, and they all yelled "Hey Ed!" When I asked them to sign the petition, one of them yelled, "Yea, I'll sign. We'll get out of class!" The others, who initially had looked indecisive, immediately joined him in signing the petition.

As I turned to leave the room, I noticed that Charles Crowe, who was one of the JAs (and who happened to be black), was standing in the doorway. We walked out together, and he explained that earlier during the day when the news of King's assassination came over the radios, those same fellows were running up and down the hallway shouting: "Martin Luther Coon been shot! Martin Luther Coon been shot!" Crowe had seen me go into that room alone, so he figured that he had better come down in case things turned nasty and I needed some help.

Charles Crowe[44]

The other black student in Blue Ridge (Homer Williams) later observed that it was probably difficult for most of the white guys not to sign the petition, because of the sad almost tearful expression on my face. He was probably right because I knew how much Dr. King was hated. In fact, approximately a year before, a kindly middle-aged white man whom I worked with as high school student in

[44]Photograph courtesy The Berea College Digital Collections, Berea Chimes Online, 1968, p. 55.

South Carolina, told me matter-of-factly that "somebody ought to shoot him!" Now, I thought, they have finally done it, and I was deeply hurt, but not surprised.

Homer Williams[45]

After gathering the signatures, I went to my room on the second floor of Blue Ridge and turned on my radio. My white roommate, Robert (Bob "Blues") Montgomery, was down the hall with his friends, where he usually would remain until about bedtime. We never talked much anyway. As I sat listening to the continuing news coverage of the assassination, Bob returned earlier than usual, however, and sat upon the upper bunk bed and began listening too. Neither of us said a word for a long time. Then Bob quietly asked, "Ed what did Dr. King have his Ph.D. in?" I told him that it was in Philosophy and Religion. Although those were the only words we exchanged that night, I felt that he too had been shaken and permanently changed by the events of that day.

The next day I turned the petition signatures over to Gatewood, and he indicated that President Weatherford was already leaning toward canceling classes in honor of Dr. King's funeral, and classes were indeed canceled on the day of the funeral.

Aftermath of the King Assassination

Just as the assassination of Dr. King changed the nation, it also changed Berea College. There appeared to me to be a more gradual acceptance of "black consciousness" and of the Black Student Union, by the white student body and faculty as a whole.

[45]Photograph courtesy The Berea College Digital Collections, Berea Chimes Online, 1968, p. 67.

A little over a month after the King Assassination and the ensuing national riots in the cities, the College invited the outspoken civil right activist Fannie Lou Hamer to speak at a weekly convocation. I was invited (along with Susan Smith, I believe), to meet with Ms. Hamer in the Alumni Building prior to her speech and to escort her over to Phelps Stokes Chapel, where she would speak. Of all of the persons that I have met, I am so glad that I met her. Just talking to her, one on one, about her struggles and how she was so severely beaten in jail until she developed a blood clot from which she never fully recovered, was so memorable. When she rose in the chapel and begin to speak, her delivery was totally amazing. I will never forget her visit to Berea. I know that she reached the hearts of some of the white students. Dean Sheely, a white fellow freshman from Blue Ridge Dorm, approached me after the speech and confided that he had been touched by the speech, although he didn't agree with Ms. Hamer's view about why the FBI was taking so long to find Dr. King's assassin. Ms. Hamer's view was that if it had been a black man who had killed a white leader, he would have been found immediately. Dean felt that the FBI was doing its best, so he and I agreed to disagree on that question.

Fannie Lou Hamer[46]

After Dr. King's assassination, BSU Faculty Sponsor, Dr. James Holloway invited the young black civil right activist, John Lewis (currently United States Congressman) to Berea's campus. Holloway knew Lewis, Dr. King, and other civil rights preachers through his membership in the interracial Council of Southern Churchmen. Lewis spoke to a small group of interested students in Danforth Chapel in the Draper Building. Holloway asked Lewis to address the question of "Where Do We Go From Here" in the aftermath of the King Assassination. Lewis was as passionate as ever but simply

[46]Photograph from "Freedom's Sisters Exhibition" online at: http://www.free-domssisters.com/ Courtesy the Cincinnati Museum Center; the Smithsonian Institution Traveling Exhibition Service (SITES), and the Library of Congress. There are no known restrictions on the publication of this photograph.

admitted that he did not know where we would go from here without Dr. King. Lewis left a lasting impression on my young mind.

John Lewis[47]

I also thought that I detected a growing acceptance of "black political consciousness" on campus shortly after the King assassination when our freshman class held its Spring elections for class officers for the upcoming sophomore year. Fellow black student, Susan Smith, who served with me on the Negro Studies Committee, approached me and suggested that the black freshmen ought to run someone for each of the offices. We both agreed that it was a good idea, and Susan spoke to others and we ended up with a slate of black candidates for each of the offices. Since there were only 16 black freshmen (eleven women and five men), we knew that our chances were slim, but we thought that at least one of us might win an office. Homer William, was nominated for Vice President, I think, and I was nominated for the Men's Social Chairman. Homer immediately put up a campaign poster in Blue Ridge Hall, and someone immediately burned it down.

Homer warned me that if I put up a poster, it would suffer the same fate, but I posted one anyway and it too was immediately burned down. I knew that this was partially a juvenile prank because the bulletin board in Blue Ridge was always blackened with smoke marks from where signs had been burned. I also felt, however, that this could be racially motivated since it had happened to both Homer and I, right in a row. So I decided to speak out in my own quiet way. I sit down and wrote an open letter to the dorm and entitled it in bold letters: **"Racism In Blue Ridge Dorm!"** I posted it on the bulletin board, and it was never burned down. In fact, only one white student ever mentioned it

[47]Photograph online at, http://www.nps.gov/subjects/civilrights/john-lewis.htm. Courtesy the National Park Service and Library of Congress. There are no known restrictions on the publication of this photograph.

to me, and that was Jim Justice, who told me that he didn't think much of it.

I was the only black candidate to be elected to a sophomore class position that Spring. I have often thought that my open letter placed some degree of guilt and shame on some of the white guys in Blue Ridge Hall and that some of them voted for me for that reason. I also knew, however, that Blue Ridge was only one dorm, and that I probably received votes from some of the men in Pearsons Hall which was the other freshmen men's dorm. I also was aware, that the majority of the white freshmen were women, so a number of them must have voted for me too. So this entire episode made me feel that there was indeed a changing mood on campus regarding race relations.

Sophomore class officers for 1968-69, from left: Lanny Huff, Scarlett Breeding, Shirley Dixon, Edward Smith, and Barbara Scoggins.[48]

---

[48]Photograph courtesy The Berea College Digital Collections, Berea Chimes Online, 1969, p. 92.

Assassination of Robert Kennedy

Another tragedy that occurred in the very late Spring of 1968, also affected Berea and the nation. In early June of 1968, New York Senator, Robert F. Kennedy, brother of slain President John F. Kennedy, and a friend of the civil rights movement, was assassinated while campaigning for the Democratic nomination for President in California. My older sister, Juanita, had just graduated from Berea, a few days earlier, and some members of my family were driving from the Berea/Lexington area to Chicago to visit my uncle when we heard the news of the assassination on the radio. We were distressed by this random act of violence, coming so soon after the assassination of Dr. King. When we arrived in Chicago the city was still enveloped in smoke from the riot and fires that had erupted following the King assassination back in April. As we drove up to my uncle's row house, a middle-aged black man, who lived downstairs, sat outside with a shotgun in his lap, guarding the house against potential looters. My aunt informed us that there was only one grocery store left in her Chicago neighborhood; the others had been burned. I returned to Berea to attend summer school, which turned out to be rather uneventful. Then just before the beginning of Fall classes in early September 1968, racial terror struck the Berea Community directly.

June 17, 1968 Cover of Newsweek Magazine. This issue of the magazine was devoted to the coverage of the assassination of Senator Robert F. Kennedy, a known friend of civil rights.[49]

---

[49]Magazine given to Edward Smith by freshman classmate, Jolene Martin (Benson), in 1968. Courtesy Edward Smith's Personal Collection.

Racial Terror Descends On Berea

In the late Summer of 1968, a group of National State Rights Party members, an openly racist organization supporting Alabama Governor George Wallace for President, deliberately came to Berea one weekend to antagonize the college, and the tiny black community living just outside of the town. Loudspeakers were set up in a field on Sunday morning, September 1, and racist epithets were hurled for all to hear. A small group of black men who grew tired of the harassment gathered their rifles and went to settle the matter. When the gunfire was over, one white man was dead, and one black man, Mr. Leona John Boggs (from the community), was also dead.[50]

I have always thought that Berea College was fortunate in that the Summer School had ended, and there were no African American male students on campus when the State's Right Party arrived and began its campaign of harassment. I fear that if young black men had still been on campus, some of them might have been tempted to confront the State's Rights Party bigots.

I had attended Summer School, along with my brother Odell, but we had both returned home to South Carolina before the disturbance in Berea. We read about it in our local newspaper, the Spartanburg Herald. The disturbance was national news for a number of days.

My soon to be girlfriend (and eventually my wife), arrived on campus early with her parents, and witnessed the height of the racial tensions in Berea in early September 1968. Her name is Claudette Schmidt, and she arrived on campus from Martinsville, Virginia. The following is her story of her first day at Berea, as she related it to me, and as she also related it a year later to Professor Gary English's Social Science class.

---

[50]Steven Connelly, "Racial Shooting in Berea on 1 Sep 1968," Berea Encyclopedia online blog, May 25, 2005. Connelly cites his sources as the Berea Citizen, 5 Sep 1968; 12 Sep 1968; 17 Oct 1968; 31 Oct 1968; 14 Nov 1968; and 20 Mar 1969. See this article at http://bereaencyclopedia.blogspot.com/2005/05/racial-shooting-in-berea-on-1-sep-1968.html

Claudette Schmidt[51]

Claudette and her parents left Martinsville via Greyhound Bus, which was the common mode of travel for many Berea students at that time. They left Martinsville on the weekend (a Saturday) and her father had to return to work the following Tuesday. They arrived in Berea early Sunday morning, and after having something to eat, they sit around the Carlton Restaurant (Greyhound Bus Station) for a couple of hours since very few customers were there. Then they decided to walk around the campus and headed toward the interesting looking building known as the Log House. Along the way, a car-load of young white bigots yelled the "N" word and sped away. Claudette's father picked up a rock, drew back his arm, but did not throw the stone. From the Log House, they walked over to the Edwards Building, and then returned to the Carlton. By then, it was well into the afternoon, so they begin to think of looking for a place to lodge. Since Boone Tavern was clearly visible nearby, they approached the registration desk and asked for rooms. The kindly desk clerk informed them that if Claudette knew which dorm she had been assigned to, they all could probably stay in the dormitory and save money. Claudette knew that she had been assigned to Kentucky Hall, so the desk clerk pointed out the directions, and the three of them went walking to Kentucky Hall.

---

[51]Photograph courtesy The Berea College Digital Collections, Berea Chimes Online, 1969, p. 106.

Claudette's parents, John and Lula Schmidt, accompanied her to Berea during the height racial tensions in the Summer of 1968.[52]

As they entered Kentucky Hall, they were kindly greeted by the dorm mother, Mrs. Blanche Upton, and her Junior Assistants (JA's). These very pleasant women assured Claudette and her parents that they could have rooms for the night. Claudette and her mother would share a room, and Claudette's father would be given another room.

A composite showing Kentucky Hall Dormitory Director, Mrs. Blanche Upton, at left, and five of the Junior Assistants (JA's): Janice Maddox (Harris), Alice Hill, Barbara Scoggins, Sue Greer (Styles), and Phyllis Taylor.[53]

---

[52]Photograph courtesy Claudette Schmidt's Personal Collection of Family Photographs.
[53]Photograph courtesy The Berea College Digital Collections, Berea Chimes Online, 1959, p. 86; 1968, pp. 63-65, 67.

Miss Upton then informed Claudette and her parents of the heightened racial tensions in the community. She said that she had heard that a bunch of "hippies and yippies" had come down from Cincinnati to burn the college down because they didn't like integrated schools. She also said that earlier during the day, she and one of her JAs, Janice Maddox, had slipped down to the rear of the State's Rights Party rally where they wouldn't be noticed. The hatred and bigotry that they heard stunned them. Miss Upton also said that a fellow dorm mother in James Hall had called her earlier to let her know that she had seen smoke rising in the distance. It later turned out that the smoke was coming from a fire as far away as Paris, Kentucky (51 miles), but just the sight of the smoke was enough to strike fear into the hearts of peace-loving Bereans.

Miss Upton told Claudette's father that the only weapons she had in the dorm, were an old rifle and a large machete. After inspecting the two weapons, Claudette's father (a World War II veteran who had seen the concentration camps in Europe), assured Miss Upton, that he would sit guard with the two weapons so that the women could get a good night's sleep. He placed a chair on the second floor near the stairs so that he had a clear view of the front door, and he sat guard for most of the night.

Before going to bed, Miss Upton told Claudette's parents, that they might want to take their daughter back home because no one was feeling safe in Berea. Claudette spoke up and assured her parents that she wanted to stay in Berea, and did not want to go back home. She felt that she had come too far to simply turn around and go back out of fear. With her father sitting guard, she apparently did feel safe and got a long good night's sleep; because when she awoke the next morning, her parents had already boarded the bus and were well on their way back to Martinsville.

Claudette later told me that when she related this story to Dr. Gary English's Social Science class, he apologized for the college. He said that no incoming freshmen should have had to endure that kind of tension on campus their very first day.

IV

Carrying on the Struggle:
The BSU's Steady Progress,
Fall 1968-Spring 1969

Before the black seniors graduated in June of 1968, a meeting was held to elect new BSU officers for the next school year. I recall that a departing senior James (Jim) Boulware nominated me for president, but I declined. I said that I was still just a freshman, and I suggested that a junior (rising senior) ought to lead the organization. Someone then nominated my brother, Odell Smith, who was in his junior year. He accepted the nomination and was elected President. Among the other four elected officers were three juniors (rising seniors) and one freshman (a rising sophomore). I am fairly certain that Joyce Perry (Flowers), a rising sophomore, was elected Secretary. I also believe that Peggy Sloan (Kemp), Catherine (Cathy) Scott and Henry Smith three juniors (rising seniors) were the other elected officers.[54]

Odell Smith, second President of the BSU.[55]

Incoming Freshmen Complaints

The upper-class members of the BSU generally supported the new president, Odell Smith, despite major personality differences, and the fact that he continued to openly date a white female student

[54]Except for Joyce Perry as Secretary, I am not sure what positions the other three persons held.
[55]Photograph courtesy Berea College Digital Collections, Berea Chimes Online, 1969, p. 73.

45

on campus. His dating of the white female student particularly aggravated some of the black women.[56]

Some of the incoming freshmen, however, as well as some of the older black students, had other questions about the organization. At the first BSU meeting of the semester, the freshmen members chose my future girlfriend Claudette Schmidt as their spokesperson, and raised the following two questions: What was the purpose of the BSU, and why was a white faculty member serving as the sponsor of the organization?

The answer to this last question was, of course, very simple: There were no black faculty persons. As to the first question concerning the purpose of the BSU, I am not sure if this was ever fully answered to the freshmen's satisfaction. Their major concern, in my opinion, was that since they were new to the campus, they did not want to get into any trouble that might cause their expulsion from the college, and I personally was always sympathetic to their feelings.

Claudette Schmidt, was selected the spokesperson for the black freshmen, Fall 1968[57]

---

[56]Odell's continued dating of a white female student, Susan Oliver, was seen by some of the black female students not only as hypocrisy, but also as a betrayal, since some of them were never asked out on dates due to the absurd shortage of black males on campus. This issue was raised in an open meeting when the male President of the University of Louisville BSU was invited to Berea to give advice and support. Faced with addressing this issue, and obviously feeling pressure from the irate female students, the visiting male president from Louisville, could only smile at Odell and softly agree that the black female students had a point.
[57]Photograph courtesy The Berea College Digital Collections, <u>Berea Chimes Online</u>, 1970, p. 55.

Black Students Walkout

So when classes started during the Fall of 1968, in spite of some initial discontent, the Black Student Union was a fully organized and functioning student organization, with a faculty sponsor, recognized by the college. As indicated earlier, the black students had agreed at the initial meeting of the organization in the early Spring of 1968, that there was a list of at least ten major complaints against the college:

1. the lack of discussions about race in chapel and convocations;

2. the dearth of black chapel and convocation speakers;

3. the total absence of black faculty;

4. the paltry number of black students;

5. the absence of black related courses in the curriculum;

6. subtle racist attitudes showed by well-meaning officials;

7. prejudiced white students who refused to room with blacks;

8. dorm mothers who frowned upon interracial dating;

9. the "Star Lite Hike," excluding many black freshmen women;

10. President Weatherford's well-intentioned use of term Niggra.

Therefore, in the Fall of 1968, the BSU, decided to focus on complaint #1: the lack of discussions about race in chapel and convocations; and complaint #2, the dearth of black chapel speakers. The student members of the Negro Studies Committee (Wallace Gatewood, Ann Beard, Susan Smith, and Ed Smith) had reported to the BSU in the late Spring of 1968, how these two issues had been hotly debated in the Committee. So in the Fall of 1968, the BSU decided to stage a "walk out" to protest the college's slowness in responding to these two issues.

The "walkout" proceeded quietly on November 7, 1968, with about 20 black students walking out, supported by about a half dozen whites. Reporters from the <u>Berea Citizen</u> newspaper and the <u>Pinnacle</u> (the college newspaper), interviewed BSU President Odell Smith, and the spokesperson for the white students, George

McCalister. Odell explained that the black students had walked out in protest over the College's seeming reluctance to discuss race relations in chapel and convocations; and the dearth of blacks invited to speak at chapel and convocations. George McCalister, on the other hand, told the reporters that he and the whites had walked out in support of the black students; and also to protest compulsory chapel attendance. None of the black students opposed compulsory chapel at that time, so George was clearly going out on a limb. George was a non-traditional student who lived in the married student trailers behind the Library. He was by far the oldest student at Berea and considered himself a radical, if not an "old Bolshevik,"[58] but few students took him seriously.

Growing BSU Recognition

The activism and dignity displayed in the "walkout" brought greater recognition to the BSU as a critical organization on campus. About this time, it was given office space in the Post Office Building and was also given recognition in the Homecoming Parade in mid-November.

This poster probably hung in BSU office, Fall 1968.[59]

---

[58]During the previous semester, as a delegate to the Little United Nations General Assembly, George as a Berea Soviet Delegation member, insisted on calling himself an "old Bolshevik." For more on George McCalister, see Appendix E, p. 131.
[59]Photograph courtesy The Berea College Digital Collections, Berea Chimes Online, 1969, p. 12.

BSU President Odell Smith, with fellow BSU officer, Henry Smith, and BSU Homecoming Parade car, November 1968.[60]

"We Can't Find Qualified Candidates"

The reaction to the "walkout" in the Fall Semester of 1968 was rather mild. In fact, I don't recall any angry reactions at all. There seem to be a growing recognition among the college faculty and administrators that the black students had some very valid complaints, and the college continued to take halting steps toward addressing some of those complaints.

During the previous semester (Spring Semester of 1968), the college hired its first black non-custodial staff person. She was Mrs. Callie Dean from Chicago, Illinois (originally from Richmond, Kentucky). She arrived with her three teenage daughters in the early Spring of 1968 and took up her position in the Registrar's Office. At that time, the college had only two other black staff persons,

[60]Photograph courtesy The Berea College Digital Collections, Berea Chimes Online, 1969, p. 147. Odell and Henry are giving the raised fist "black power salute" made popular by Olympic athletes John Carlos and Tommie Smith at the 1968 Mexico City Summer Olympics.

and they both worked in the Food Service kitchen. They were Mr. Alonzo Ballard and Mrs. Amanda Walker. Mr. Ballard lived just outside Berea in the black enclave of Farristown, and Mrs. Walker lived in the town of Berea, just beyond the married student trailers.

In the early Fall of 1968, the college also hired a black Admissions Recruiter, Benny Alexander (who had graduated from Berea the previous June). His role in dramatically increasing the black student enrollment the following year was probably invaluable.

Benny Alexander became the first black Admissions Recruiter, in the Fall of 1968.[61]

In addition to focusing on race relations and getting black chapel speakers invited to Berea, the BSU in the Fall and Spring of 1968-69 turned its attention to the next two items on its ten-item list of complaints: #3, the total absence of black faculty; and #4, the paltry number of black students. Regarding the absence of black faculty, there was not much the BSU could do except to reiterate its complaint. The generic answer from the administration was: "We can't find qualified candidates," to come at the low salaries that the college offered.

So with BSU President Odell Smith's approval, senior Richard Greenlee and I, volunteered to meet with Director of Admissions, Mr. Allan Morreim, to discuss the problem of recruiting black students. The meeting proved to be very fruitful and opened my eyes to the difficulty of recruiting. Prior to the meeting, Mr. Morreim had pulled the folders of two black applicants from the year that I was accepted into Berea (1967). I had no idea that these two black students (whom I had attended high school with), had ever applied

---

[61]Photograph courtesy The Berea College Digital Collections, <u>Berea Chimes Online</u>, 1968, p. 21.

to Berea. I assumed that Mr. Morreim thought that I might know these students, so he pulled their folders in order to give me some idea of why they had not been accepted. The basic problem was their SAT scores, which were below 600, and therefore considered "Higher Risk." Mr. Morreim explained that students scoring below 600 would probably simply drop out on their own accord, so it would be unfair to accept them in the first place. Up to that time (1968), Berea did not take Higher Risk students. Mr. Morreim was later proven to be correct, in my opinion.

Mr. Morreim, instead, strongly encouraged Richard Greenlee and me, to get the word out to the BSU members to urge any black high school students that they might know, to apply to Berea. The BSU students took Mr. Morreim's message to heart, and they (the BSU students) in some measure, contributed to the doubling of the black student population at Berea the following school year (Fall Semester 1969).

Mr. Allan Morreim[62]

Faculty Debate Increasing Black Enrollment

In the meantime, the college faculty and administration were wrestling with the need to increase the college's black student enrollment. The college's Admissions Committee, reacting primarily to the recommendations of the Issues and Values Committee presented 4 proposals to the College Faculty Meeting on April 5, 1969.

The last sentence of Proposal Number 3 called for more extensive

[62]Photograph courtesy The Berea College Digital Collections, Berea Chimes Online, 1966, p. 125.

recruiting of black students over the next four years until black enrollment at the college would become equal to the percentage of blacks in the national population, which at that time was about 11 or 12 percent.

As soon as that proposal came up for consideration, Mr. Paul Hager, Director of Counseling and Testing, rose and moved to amend the proposal to state that the increase in black enrollment should "double" the national average. Dr. Richard Drake of the History Department immediately offered to amend Mr. Hager's amendment to say "substantially higher" than the national average.

Dr. George Parker of the Philosophy and Religion Department then offered an amendment to simply remove the last sentence, and that there be no mention of a goal. He felt that "progress" was being made, and that since there were no black faculty persons and just a tiny local black community, the increase should be more gradual.

Dr. Norris Woodie of the Philosophy and Religion Department then rose and stated his opposition to Dr. Parker's amendment. He said that the proposal under consideration would not establish a quota, "but would give us a target to aim at, i.e., a goal to be achieved." Dean Louis Smith stated his opposition to the idea of a goal or quota. Dr. Dorothy Tredennick of the Art Department immediately responded to Dean Smith by stating that: "We have been trying to move gradually since 1950 in order to increase black faculty, and look where we are now."

President Weatherford stated his reservations. He was afraid that both the Faculty and Trustees might react negatively to "the words quota or goal in connection with our commitment to interracial education, as we have done with our Appalachian commitment." Dr. Parker's amendment was then voted upon and passed "by a two to one margin, the final vote count being 74-38," so the original proposal was rejected.

A composite showing Professors Hager, Drake, Parker, Woodie, Vice President Smith, Professor Tredennick, and President Weatherford. In a faculty meeting on April 5, 1969, these seven persons debated the last sentence of a proposal (and an amendment to that sentence) that would have dramatically increased black enrollment at Berea College. The controversial last sentence of the proposal was removed by an overwhelming vote.[63]

[63]Photographs from Berea College Yearbook, 1971 (volume is not online), pp. 25, 45, 51. Original volume courtesy Claudette Schmidt's Personal Collection. The other photographs are courtesy The Berea College Digital Collections, Berea Chimes Online, 1962, p. 68, 72; and 1969, p. 25.

Parker Amends Admissions Committee Proposal

Faculty Rejects Black Enrollment Increase

On Monday night, April 5, the College Faculty held its regularly scheduled monthly meeting. The most important and controversial matter of business of the three hour session was concern for the college's interracial commitment with regard to the black student enrollment. At this time the Admissions Committee, acting primarily as a result of an earlier recommendation from the Issues and Values staff, made the following proposal:

1. The establishment of a post titled Director of Black Studies, whose responsibility it would be to coordinate those aspects of Berea's program presently devoted to a study of black culture and history and to offer leadership in the expansion of those offerings.

2. The continuation and intensification of the effort to engage black faculty with the institutional goal of achieving approximately the same ratio to black faculty members as that within the student body. Although the realities of the market pose tremendous difficulties, we affirm this ratio as an eventual goal.

3. The establishment of an admissions effort which would support more intensive recruiting for black students in the context of finding the best students whose personal situation indicates the greatest need, with particular emphasis on those from Southern Appalachia. During the next four years the college should enroll a student body whose American black complement shall at a minimum be equal to the percentage of the national population which is black.

4. The establishment of procedures designed to meet the educational problem which motivated the Issues and Values staff recommendation:

a. Teams of black upperclass students who would work with Issues and Values sections during their discussions of the black and white issue.

b. Black citizens from the area who could help our students come to a better understanding of the black experience in America—each spending a day on campus meeting with sections from the Issues and Values class.

It was immediately decided by the body that each of the four points of the proposal should be considered separately before a final vote on the matter in its entirety. The first two points were accepted with very little discussion concerning their function or purpose, although several people did volunteer brief comments in relation to their content.

As soon as the third point was open for consideration, Paul Hager moved that the increase would be "double that" of the national average. Richard Drake made a motion to amend Hager's amendment to read "substantially higher" than that of the national average. Rapid and intense debate ensued as a result of these two motions; numerous faculty members and administrators offered varying and conflicting suggestions, details, and information.

After the conversation had continued for some time, George Parker made a "substitute amendment" that the last sentence of the third point be omitted from the content of the proposal. Weatherford, who was conducting the meeting, ruled that the "substitute amendment" would be voted upon before the original amendments of Hager and Drake.

Parker explained his reasons for making this motion by presenting the idea that there are "other matters" in the Berea community which need to be worked with before any change in present college admission policy should be made. He specifically pointed out the problems which arise due to the small number of black residents in Berea; he mentioned the possibility that a large number of black students on a campus in a nearly all-white community might not lead to good relations between the two groups. He also concerned himself with the fact that there are presently no black faculty members at Berea; in connection with this problem he stated that it might be "unwise" to increase black enrollment before increasing the number of black instructors. It was also his opinion that these problems are being worked on in a "significant way" at the present time, and that "progress is being made." He concluded by asserting that we need to actualize these and other changes before we undertake any policy which "would upset the present balance" of our situation.

Norris Woodie then requested and received the floor at which time he read a statement which opposed the motion to delete this sentence. Woodie drew an analogy between the early civil rights laws and the proposal calling for a significant black increase. He stated that an Amendment to the U.S. Constitution had assured blacks of their freedoms in the early 1800's, but pointed out that it was not until over a century later that blacks actually were able to secure some of these rights when the federal government began to pass and to enforce civil rights laws. He likened this information to the ideal that Berea should actualize its interracial commitment in a similar manner. Woodie also talked about the difference between a QUOTA and a GOAL, stating that the proposal under consideration would not establish a quota, but would give us a "target to aim at," i.e., a goal to be achieved.

At a later point in the meeting Louis Smith voiced opposition to this line of thinking, stating that "a goal when achieved becomes a quota. It would not be difficult to establish a quota, but not at a rate which will double our number of blacks in a short period of time. Let us not put ourselves in a kind of quota, but accept his (Parker's) motion. We must move gradually."

Dorothy Tredennick immediately responded to Smith, saying: "We have been trying to move gradually since 1950 in order to increase black faculty, and look where we are now."

Willis Weatherford also had some interesting observations to express. One of his more pressing points of concern was reflected in his statement that, (in connection with black increase,) "I would hope that it would help—but I am afraid it would hurt." Weatherford went on to explain that the college could not "undertake abrupt changes," or "undergo a turnabout" in college policy without the "overwhelming" support of both faculty and trustees. He said that he was afraid of the words "quota" or "goal" in connection with the interracial commitment, as we have done with our Appalachian commitment.

Eventually it was decided to end discussion on Parker's amendment and to vote. It passed by a two-to-one margin, the final vote count being 74-38. The faculty then quickly decided to send the fourth point back to the Issues and Values staff, in order that the staff could consider these suggestions as well as react to them.

Newspaper article from April 1969 on the joint Admissions Committee/Issues and Values Staff proposal on increasing black student enrollment. A radical amendment to Proposal 3 calling for the establishment of a numerical goal was voted down "as a quota" at the Faculty Meeting held April 5, 1969. In the meantime, the Admissions Office along with the BSU were already involved in an intensive effort to recruit black students.[64]

[64]Courtesy Claudette Schmidt's Personal Scrapbook, 1968-1972.

Growth of Black Cultural Events

The BSU as a cultural organization also continued to develop during the Fall and Spring Semesters of 1968-69. During the late spring and summer of 1968, some of the black female students had decided to become "Big Sisters" to some of the incoming freshmen women that they knew would be arriving in the Fall of 1968. So as "Big Sisters" they wrote letters to some of the incoming freshmen women in an effort to form friendships and extend warm welcomes prior to their arrival on campus.

Some of the black female students also decided among themselves to make other plans to warmly welcome the incoming freshmen. So upon the arrival of the freshman class in the Fall of 1968, Brenda Stuart (Harris) led a welcome tour of the campus. Daily Williams (Smith) led a welcome hike of the campus that including the lovely Berea cemetery.

Brenda Stuart[65]   Daily Williams[66]

Eva Reed and Gay Nell Bell introduced the freshmen women in the Fall of 1968 to their gospel singing group, the forerunner of the Black Ensemble. They continued to sing in the private room inside the Alumni Building that housed the piano, and they also continued to sing in their dorm rooms.

---

[65]Photograph courtesy The Berea College Digital Collections, Berea Chimes Online, 1968, p. 52.
[66]Photograph courtesy The Berea College Digital Collections, Berea Chimes Online, 1969, p. 89.

Eva Reed[67]   Gay Nell Bell[68]

The first official black cultural event was organized by BSU women in the Spring of 1969. It was known as an "Osun Dudu" which in Yoruba simply means "dark or black." It can also be translated to mean "Black Month" or the very popular product sold internationally today as "Black Soap" or "African Black Soap."[69] Osun was also "one of the Orisa (the traditional deities of the Yoruba people)."[70] The title of the event may have been borrowed from one of the African students present on campus that school year, Peter Aidoo, from Ghana.[71]

The women, led by senior Geneva Isom, sewed dashikis for all of the men who were interested in attending the event. That was the only dashiki that I ever owned, and I kept it for many years afterward. We were asked to volunteer to solicit donations from faculty in order to pay for the event.

I remember approaching BSU Sponsor, Dr. James Holloway, about a donation. He was not interested in how we "sing and dance," but offered to give a donation to bring in speakers if the BSU was so inclined. He pointed out that some of the faculty at Berea were "only" interested in how "blacks sang and dance." He suggested that I ask his good friend Dr. Robert Menefee, whom he

---

[67]Photograph courtesy The Berea College Digital Collections, Berea Chimes Online, 1970, p 55.
[68]Photograph courtesy The Berea College Digital Collections, Berea Chimes Online, 1970, p. 44.
[69]Church Missionary Society, A Dictionary of the Yoruba Language. Lagos, Nigeria: Church Missionary Society Bookshop, 1913, pp. 15 (29), 93 (107). See online at http://edeyoruba.com/uploads/3/0/0/1/3001787/yoruba_dictionary.pdf and http://duduosum.com/order/shop/dudu-osun-black-soap/
[70]https://en.wikipedia.org/wiki/Osun_(state)
[71]The only other African student on campus that school year (1968-69) was Richard Marange from Rhodesia.

jokingly described as a "good liberal," and who would probably give a donation. I believe I did approach Dr. Menefee, and I believe he did indeed make a donation to the event. I assume other faculty members also made donations. The event, was, of course, open to all students and faculty. The event went over very well, probably because as Holloway had indicated, it was less threatening and boring than a political speech or a discussion of racial issues, and everyone did indeed have a good time.

Geneva Isom[72]

Addressing Racism: "Telling It Like It Is!"

The Fall Semester of 1968 and the Spring Semester of 1969 continued to be exciting times at Berea. The open discussions in the Alumni Building Lounge on the issue of "race," which had begun in the late Spring of 1968, continued sporadically into the Fall, and on into the Spring of 1969. They were not BSU sponsored, and I am not sure if the gatherings were even well planned, although some faculty members usually became involved in the discussions. At one such memorable event, Dr. Charles Harris, the College Physician, and Dr. Holloway (the BSU Sponsor) engaged in an interesting discussion regarding the idea of "color-blindness" in race relations. Dr. Harris argued that when a patient sat down before him in his office, he did not "see race" at all; instead, he saw another human being. Dr. Holloway, on the other hand, suggested that the idea of

[72]Photograph courtesy The Berea College Digital Collections, Berea Chimes Online, 1969, p. 62.

"color-blindness" was a great theory, philosophy, and practice "ten years ago" in the 1950s. Holloway argued that the situation had now changed. Blacks were now demanding that whites not only see their color but above all respect their color, as expressed in a popular song of 1968: "Say It Loud, I'm Black and I'm Proud."

Dr. James Holloway[73] Dr. Charles Harris, M.D.[74]

In another open discussion in the Alumni Building Lounge on the issue of race, in the Spring of 1969, I was surprised to see my old freshmen roommate Bob Montgomery present. We had never talked about the issue as roommates. So I was even more surprised when Bob took to the floor and stated to all of the whites present that: "We have told the blacks what to do for all of these years, so why don't we just shut up and listen to them for a change."

At the end of the school year in June 1969, the college invited Dr. Joseph Taylor, a black Sociology Professor and Dean of the School of Liberal Arts at the University of Indiana (Indianapolis campus), to be its commencement speaker. Dr. Taylor's grandmother had been among the black students at Berea prior to the passage of the state's segregationist Day Law in 1904. My brother, BSU President, Odell Smith, was among the graduates of 1969, so I stayed for the commencement exercises at Indian Fort Amphitheatre and heard Dr. Taylor's speech. The focus of Dr. Taylor's speech was on "racial prejudice" and the dangers of pre-judging people. It was indeed a speech for America in the late 1960s; a speech for the "climate of the times." Following the speech, Odell's future father-in-law, Mr. Leonard Hale, who attended the commencement from Lexington, Kentucky, expressed his heartfelt reactions to my father (Odell

---

[73]Photograph courtesy The Berea College Digital Collections, Berea Chimes Online, 1966, p. 137.
[74]Photograph from Berea College Yearbook, 1971 (volume is not online), p. 40. Original volume courtesy Claudette Schmidt's Personal Collection.

Smith, Sr.) and to me. According to Mr. Hale, Dr. Taylor in his speech had "laid it all out" and was simply "telling it like it is!"

Dr. Joseph Taylor[75]

---

[75]During the commencement exercises Dr. Taylor was awarded an honorary Doctor of Laws Degree from Berea College. A year later he would become the first black member of the Berea College Board of Trustees since James Bond, who had served from 1896-1914. He also became a friend of the BSU, and I considered him a personal friend. See Appendix J. Photograph courtesy IUPUI University Library Special Collections and Archives, and Inside IUPUI, online newsletter, February 14, 2014. See online at: http://inside.iupui.edu/features/stories/2014-02-18-feature-taylor-symposium.shtml

New Sponsorship:
The BSU, Mr. Marshall, and the Triumph
of Black Culture, Fall 1969-Spring 1970

Prior to graduation exercises in the late Spring of 1969, the BSU elected it officers for the next school year. A freshman (rising sophomore) Billy Foster, was elected President. This was the first time a person who was not a senior or rising senior, had been elected President of the organization. Billy, who had been extremely critical of the BSU all during his freshman year, now ironically found himself as leader of the organization.[76] I cannot recall all of the four other elected officers, but at least three of them were Homer Williams and myself (two rising juniors), and Mary Palmer (Dennis), who was a rising sophomore.

Billy Foster, third President of the BSU.[77]

---

[76]In addition to hearing complaints directly from Billy during the previous school year (1968-1969), I was often stopped by a white student known as "Maw," who was a JA in Billy's freshman dormitory, Blue Ridge Hall. Maw would tell me what "Billy and Charlie" [Billy Foster and Charlie Crowe], were saying about the BSU. Maw's gossip was always negative.

[77]Photograph courtesy The Berea College Digital Collections, Berea Chimes Online, 1970, p. 52.

The Arrival of the Black Counselor

During the Summer of 1969, I had the opportunity to attend the Harvard-Yale-Columbia Intensive Summer Studies Program (ISSP). It was a program sponsored by the three Ivy League universities, where students from primarily historical black colleges were given intensive summer training in preparation for entry into future graduate and professional schools. Berea was one of only 8 predominately white southern colleges included in the program, while 27 historically black colleges and universities were included. The program also had a faculty component, known as the Harvard Summer School Faculty Audit Program (FAP). Select faculty members from the participating colleges attended the Summer School, where they audited courses.

Dr. John Crowden, from Berea's Sociology Department, attended the Harvard Summer School's FAP during the Summer of 1969. I would often pause outside the FAP dorm and talk with him and several other visiting faculty persons since they seemed to be interested in chatting with passing students.

Dr. John Crowden[78]

One day while we were chatting, Dr. Crowder, told me smilingly that his wife had informed him that the new black Counselor had arrived in Berea with his family, and was "fitting in just fine;" he was "teaching Sunday School." The new Counselor was Mr. Melvin Marshall.

---

[78]Photograph courtesy The Berea College Digital Collections, <u>Berea Chimes Online</u>, 1966, p. 138.

Mr. Melvin Marshall, first black
Counselor, Summer-Fall, 1969[79]

Mr. Marshall was hired as a college Counselor in the Office of
Counseling and Testing, which was headed at that time by Mr.
Paul Hager. Although Mr. Marshall was a Counselor; during the
Fall of 1969, he was also given the responsibility of supervising
and grading the first "African History" course offered at Berea. The
course was a tele-lecture given via telephone by Dr. Okon Uya,
from the University of Wisconsin at Madison. Dr. Uya delivered the
lecture from Madison, while Mr. Marshall supervised the class at
Berea, and worked with Dr. Uya in grading the final exam.[80]

A Doubling of My People

As was stated earlier, although the first black Admissions Recruiter,
Benny Alexander, had remained with the college for only one year,
his efforts during the Fall of 1968 and Spring of 1969 helped bring
about a dramatic increase of the black student population in the
Fall of 1969.

In addition to the recruiting efforts of Benny Alexander, the
efforts of BSU members also contributed to the increase in black
students. I personally accepted Admissions Director Morreim's
advice to help recruit black students. Therefore, when I heard that
my cousin and fellow church member, Cynthia Gaffney (House) was

[79]Photograph from Berea College Yearbook, 1971 (volume is not online), p. 45.
Original volume courtesy Claudette Schmidt's Personal Collection.
[80]Several years later (in 1973), I finally met Dr. Uya in Washington, D.C., where he
had begun a professorship at Howard University.

considering Berea, I urged her to please come, because we needed black students, and she was indeed among the black freshmen who arrived in the Fall of 1969.

Cynthia Gaffney[81]

Therefore, the combined recruiting efforts of Benny Alexander and BSU members, along with the encouragement of Admissions Director Morreim, paid off big dividends in the Fall of 1969. The black student population of Berea more than doubled, increasing from 57 to 125 students.

So when the returning black students (sophomores, juniors, and seniors) arrived back on campus in the Fall of 1969, they were met by a multitude of new black students, who tended to hang out in the Alumni Building sometimes crowding the passageways. A few were transfers, but most were freshmen. The transfer students were rather mature, as would be expected of college students. The freshmen women in general, were also rather mature. Some of the freshmen students, however, tended to run in packs and were rather outspoken and loud. Some were from large urban areas, like Chicago, Cincinnati, Dayton, Baltimore, Washington, DC, Louisville, Knoxville, and Birmingham.[82] Some were from smaller towns but seemed to have adopted a more urban persona. Some of the incoming freshmen males, for example, were sexually explicit in their conversations with, and expressions toward the incoming

---

[81]Photograph courtesy The Berea College Digital Collections, Berea Chimes Online, 1970, p. 60. It was understandable at this period of time, that my cousin was also suspicious of the use of the word "black." Although she warmly assured me that she would attend Berea, she also warned that "they better not call me black!"
[82]Berea, of course, already had black students from the major cities of Birmingham, Knoxville, and Louisville, but the overwhelming majority of its black students had previously come from smaller cities and towns.

female students.[83]   Many did not appear at all to *epitomize* the traditional small-town black and white Berea student.

Some of the incoming freshmen (males and females) were "Higher Risk," and as Director of Admissions, Morreim, had predicted, some of these students did not last long. Some of the young women left rather quickly within the first year. Some of the male students hung on a little longer but departed within the first two years.

Mr. Allan Morreim[84]

Mr. Marshall's Crucial Role

As was indicated earlier, the new black Counselor, Mr. Melvin Marshall, had arrived with his family during the Summer of 1969 and gotten settled in. At this critical moment in the history of the BSU, he immediately reached out to the black students and very early on invited the officers of the BSU to dinner at his home.

---

[83]Some of the freshmen males, for example, derided the freshmen females in James Hall, as being "virgin cock mouths," a term that most of us small-town naive upperclassmen did not even know the meaning. In retaliation, the harassed young women, led by their JA, cut out small signs with the derogatory words written on them, and proudly wore them to food service meals each day, probably never knowing the exact meaning of those words.
[84]Photograph courtesy The Berea College Digital Collections, <u>Berea Chimes Online</u>, 1968, p.121.

Mr. Melvin Marshall[85]

The new incoming students had very few questions about the BSU. I think they simply assumed that the BSU had been around for quite a while. They also probably assumed that Mr. Marshall had been around for some time. Most of them probably had no idea that prior to their arrival, Berea had had a very tiny black student population.

Mr. Marshall enthusiastically assumed the role of BSU Sponsor and became far more involved with the black students than Dr. Holloway ever was. Over time, some of the students, both male, and female, virtually took up residence at his house. His home was always open, and he and his family encouraged students to visit. This was quite beneficial since many of the incoming freshmen, indeed, needed some type of parental guidance.

[85]Photograph from Berea College Yearbook, 1972 (volume is not online), p. 28. Original volume courtesy Claudette Schmidt's Personal Collection.

The Triumph of Black Culture

Mr. Marshall proved to be an inspirational cultural leader. He, along with the senior student, Charles Crowe, formally organized the Black Ensemble in the Fall of 1969. Later, Mr. Marshall, along with Mr. Paul Power, Director of the College Theatre known as the TAB, organized a traveling theater adaptation of James Baldwin's "The Amen Corner", in the Spring of 1970.

The Berea College Black Ensemble, formally organized and directed by Mr. Melvin Marshall, performs in the Alumni Building Lounge in 1970.[86]

The Berea College Black Ensemble, ca. 1970-71.[87]

---

[86]Photograph courtesy The Berea College Digital Collections, <u>Berea Chimes Online</u>, 1970, p. 115.
[87]Photograph courtesy The Berea Digital Collections, <u>Berea College History You Tube</u>. See online at: https://www.youtube.com/watch?v=5Xvl8ceFoR4

BEREANS PRESENT "AMEN CORNER" AT TALLEDEGA

Mary Palmer as Sister Margaret

On Palm Sunday weekend a group of Berea students traveled some four hundred miles to Talledega College, a small, predominately black, liberal arts college in Talledega, Alabama. The students were cast members for the first full-length dramatic production with an all-black cast to be presented at Berea. The production, James Baldwin's *Amen Corner*, deals with the conflicts between a small Harlem storefront church congregation and its spiritual leader, Sister Margaret, played by *Mary Palmer*, '72. The drama was presented at Berea in conjunction with the new Black Literature course, taught by Dr. Dorothy Brown.

The group, under the direction of *Paul Power*, '58, director of the Berea College Dramatics Laboratory, and Melvin Marshall of Counseling and Testing Service, traveled to Talledega to do a performance on invitation from Dr. Clara Chassell Cooper, chairman of the Berea psychology department from 1952 to 1961, and now the chairman of the psychology department at Talledega. Mrs. Cooper had heard of the presentation of *Amen Corner* at Berea's Tabernacle, February 7, 1970, and invited the group to perform for a special chapel service at the Alabama college.

The eleven principal cast members along with three student technical workers made the trip. Members of the cast were: *Mary Palmer*, '72, *Ruthaleen Henderson*, '72, *Eva Reed*, '71, *Claudette Schmidt*, '72, *David Frison*, '73, *Delphina Hopkins*, '73, *Edsel Massey*, '72, *Eugene Kelley*, '72, *Yuvonne Haynes*, '72, *Gay Nell Bell*, '71, *Mildred Pearson*, '71; technicians: *Glen Miracle*, '73, *Sharon Osolnik*, '72, and *Drucilla Kelly*, '73.

Music for the production, which on the Berea campus had been provided by a "congregation" composed of additional cast members, was performed by the Talledega College Choir. The Berea students, as guests of the Talledega Psychology Club, toured the campus on Saturday, and presented *Amen Corner* on Palm Sunday night in Talledega's DeForest Chapel. —   , '72

Mary Palmer as the female spiritual leader, Sister Margaret, in James Baldwin's the "Amen Corner" at Talladega College.[88]

---

[88] Courtesy Claudette Schmidt's Personal Scrapbook, 1968-72.

THE PSYCHOLOGY CLUB

Presents

JAMES BALDWIN'S "AMEN CORNER"

By

THE BEREA PLAYERS

Of

BEREA COLLEGE

In

De Forest Chapel

Talladega College, Talladega, Alabama

March 22, 1970

Page 1 of Program for the "Amen Corner" at Talladega College, 1970.[89]

---

[89]Courtesy Claudette Schmidt's Personal Scrapbook, 1968-72.

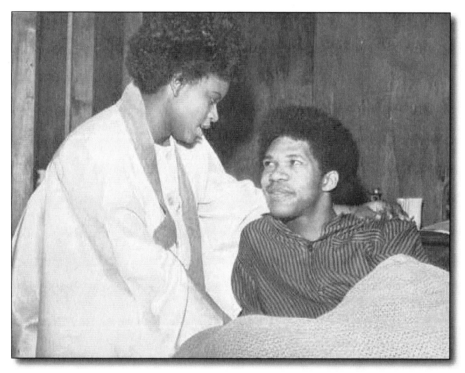

Mary Palmer and Eugene Kelley in "The Amen Corner" at Berea.[90]

[90]Photograph courtesy The Berea College Digital Collections, <u>Berea Chimes Online</u>, 1970, p. 130.

Page 1 of the Program for the very first concert given by the Black Ensemble on May 10, 1970, after which dinner was served at President Weatherford's home.[91]

The BSU Less Independent

During this period (Fall 1969-Spring 1970), the BSU became "less independent" as a student-led organization, as the overwhelming majority of the students naturally looked to Mr. Marshall for direction and inspiration. There still were no black faculty or administrators present, so we all appreciated finally having a black authority figure on campus. Therefore, he became the inspirational leader of the BSU with a primary focus on its cultural development. It was probably at the suggestion of Mr. Marshall that the BSU began holding its annual "Miss BSU Pageant" in the Spring of 1970, at which Yvonne Haynes (Greenlee) was crowned the first "Miss BSU."

So from the Fall Semester of 1969 through the Fall Semester of 1970, the BSU became less of a political organization and more distinctively a social and cultural organization, as its constitution had envisioned. Mr. Marshall said to me several times, that: "There are people around here [with talent] who can do things if you all will let them."

As an officer of the BSU, I remember trying to think of political issues that I could interest BSU President Billy Foster to examine. One idea that I clearly remember, was to get the BSU on record for giving some form of symbolic support to Black Panther co-founder Bobby Seale, who was chained and gagged in a Chicago courtroom.

In the Fall of 1969, Seale was on trial in the infamous "Chicago Eight" case. He and 7 others were accused of "conspiracy" to cross state lines to ferment riot during the 1968 Democratic Convention in Chicago. When Seale refused to sit down and stay quiet in the courtroom, Judge Julius Hoffman, ordered that he be bound to his seat and gagged.

The sight of Seale being bound and gagged in the courtroom incensed many people and the charge of "conspiracy" seemed ridiculous to many others. I informed BSU President Billy Foster of my idea, and with his approval, I wrote up a petition and gathered signatures from fellow BSU members protesting the treatment of Seale.

Over the years, I had forgotten about this petition until the National Archives sought a security clearance for me as one of its archivists in 1992. The clearance was granted, but the adjudicator of the clearance laughingly informed me that the FBI had reported that in 1969, I had written a petition and gathered signatures at Berea College in support of Bobby Seale. By 1992, Seale was a law abiding Professor in the African American Studies Department at Temple University in Philadelphia, so the information was no longer relevant; but it would have been quite relevant back in 1969. I now know that the FBI monitored all college BSUs during the late 1960s through its COINTELPRO (Counterintelligence) program.

The Arrest of 3 Students: "Let My People Go!"

At the urging of Mr. Marshall, the BSU did exert itself "politically" in one very important event during the Spring Semester of 1970. Late one night, Mr. Marshall arrived at Bingham Hall, where most of the black juniors and seniors, were living and informed us that three young black freshmen, Glen Gore, Wayne Summerville, and William Turpin, had been arrested downtown.[92]

The incident was due in part to local young white men, called "scoads" who traveled in cars down the main street of Berea and openly harassed both white and black students by yelling and threatening them. I had only heard of one incident in which a student had been physically attacked. I had been told that former College President Francis Hutchins' son had been attacked some years before my arrival on campus in 1967. I personally had never worried about the "scoads" because growing up in upstate South Carolina, being yelled at by passing whites was a common occurrence. When the new crop of black students entered Berea in the Fall of 1969, however, some of the black men began carrying sticks when they would venture downtown at night to a movie or to buy food.

On the night of their arrest, Gore, Summerville, and Turpin had gone downtown to the convenient store to purchase food. Summerville was carrying a stick, just in case he encountered "scoads." A worker in the store noticed that Summerville was carrying a stick, so he called his father who was a town policeman,

[92]The arrests occurred on the night of March 1, 1970. Gore and Summerville, were both from Mount Hope, West Virginia, near Beckley, although Gore often said that he spent a lot of time in Washington, DC. Turpin was from Cincinnati.

and reported the violation. Carrying a stick was against the law within the town, but the black male students did not know this. When the police arrived, the three men were searched, and a pistol was found on Glen Gore. All three men were arrested and taken to the town jail. They were given a chance to make a phone call, and, of course, they called Mr. Marshall.

When Mr. Marshall arrived at Bingham Hall late that night, he challenged the black men of Bingham Hall by saying: "They [the arrested men] are all part of you, so what are you going to do about it?" The seven black men of Bingham Hall (along with two others who were visiting from another dorm) reacted swiftly, by making signs and setting up a picket line in front of Lincoln Hall the next morning.[93]

---

[93]The seven junior and senior men from Bingham Hall were: Donnie Buchanan, William (Bill) Churchill, Charles Crowe, James Duckett, Thomas Hutchins, James Lewis, and myself. We were joined by Jack Miller and Earl Mitchell, two returning Army veterans, who lived in Howard Hall, but often visited Bingham Hall.

Black Students at Berea Occupy President's Office to Protest Arrests and to Express Other Grievances

A peaceful, 22-hour sit-in at Berea College President Willis D. Weatherford's office by black students of the college on March 2-3 was more than a protest against the arrest of three black students by Berea city police.

Although the demonstration followed the March 1 arrest of three students, one on charges of carrying a concealed deadly weapon and another for "carrying a weighted club within a crowded supermarket," the more than 80 black students who participated in the sit-in at Pres. Weatherford's office were attempting to bring about some communication. Melvin L. Marshall of Berea's counseling and testing service, said. Marshall who is adviser to the Black Student Union chapter at Berea, also said the "confrontation" between Pres. Weatherford and the students concerned the "needs of students on campus and the desire for security." The students said there was a good deal of harassment of college students, black and white, by townspeople and by "out-of-town" persons.

In the March 1 arrest, Glen Gore, a freshman from Mount Hope, W. Va., was charged with carrying a concealed deadly weapon, a .22 caliber pistol, found on him by city police. Wayne E. Summerville, also a freshman from Mount Hope, was arrested on the weighted club charge. A third student, William M. Turpin, a freshman from Cincinnati, was taken into custody by police but was released after a charge of disorderly conduct was dropped.

Berea police stopped and arrested the three black students

Members of the Black Student Union occupy President Weatherford's office to express grievances

after receiving a telephone call from a grocery store in the West End of Berea. A clerk at the store said three black youths had been in the store and one was carrying a "weighted club."

Members of the Black Student Union charged that the arrests were examples of "flagrant racism" and said the students would not have been arrested if they had been white. The three students who had been arrested appeared in Berea City Police Court Monday morning, March 2. Charges were dismissed formally against Turpin, and the cases of Gore and Summerville, both thought to have been felonies, were referred to the Madison County grand jury. The Berea court does not have jurisdiction over felonies. Both Gore and Summerville waived the right of attorney in the police court hearing. When the two students appeared before the grand jury, they were represented by an attorney. Marshall said he doubted that the students were fully aware of their rights before the police court hearing. After being bound over to the grand jury, the students posted bond and were released on their own recognizance.

Earlier in the year, in January, a white Berea College student had been arrested by city police and charged with carrying a concealed deadly weapon. The charge later was amended and the student fined $10 for disorderly conduct and $25.50 for discharging firearms within the city limits. The case was heard in Berea Police Court. A college regulation prohibits students from possessing firearms while in residency on the campus.

Shortly after the hearing in police court, black students protesting the arrests marched to the Berea City Hall. Some carried signs protesting the handling of the situation. The students were met by Mayor C. C. Hensley, Police Court Judge George S. Noss, the Berea police force and several county and state law enforcement personnel.

Previously the black students had met with the mayor and city officials to discuss the problems of harassment. Students told Hensley tensions between students and townspeople were increasing. Hensley replied that he would do what he could to ease tensions. Both Gore and Summerville said they had been carrying weapons to protect themselves after repeated harassment. The two students said they and some friends had been harassed by some white youths in a car shortly before being arrested.

After the march to City Hall, black students returned to the campus, first parading around Lincoln Hall and through Hutchins Library before coming to Pres. Weatherford's office. Pres. Weatherford met the students in his office and discussed student grievances. Marshall said black students went to Pres. Weatherford "since he is president and would have more push in initiating action to secure fair treatment for the arrested students." During the day Pres. Weatherford and students held three discussions to promote communication. At 2:30 p.m. Monday Pres. Weatherford left his office and the students remained. Marshall said the students "planned to stay in the office to get the satisfaction they thought was de-

10

Page 10 of an article in the May-June issue of <u>The Berea Alumnus</u> with a photograph showing the occupation of the President's Office in March 1970.[94]

[94]Courtesy Claudette Schmidt's Personal Scrapbook, 1968-72.

77

sirable and to be assured something would be done about the arrested students."

Before leaving his office Pres. Weatherford read to the black students portions of the college policy concerning the unauthorized occupation of campus buildings. A statement dealing with the rights and responsibilities of students had been formulated by several faculty members during the summer of 1969 and presented to the Cabinet for tentative approval. The statement was approved by the General Faculty at its first meeting in the fall of the 1969-70 academic year and adopted as a college regulation. The regulation was printed in the Student Handbook which was given to all students at the start of the academic year.

In the wording of the regulation, "the following activities are not acceptable because they prevent or impede the performance of the essential educational tasks of the college and are incompatible with the shared purposes of an academic community: Deliberate interference with academic freedom and freedom of speech; violence against any member or guest of the college community; interference with the freedom of movement of any member or guest of the college community; damage of college property and unauthorized entry or occupation of college facilities; and obstruction of the normal processes and activities essential to the college community." Violators, according to the regulation, are subject "to appropriate discipline within the full range of disciplinary measures including expulsion."

Pres. Weatherford informed the black students of the college regulation and of the possible disciplinary measures and said he would have to invoke the regulation sometime in the future if the students chose not to leave his office. "I looked upon the occupation as a continuing conversation and did not wish to invoke the policy for the well-being of the college and community. The students felt they were in a tough spot; they felt three of their number were being unfairly treated. It was my judgment that as soon as the students realized fair treatment was being given, they would leave on their own accord," Pres. Weatherford said.

Although Pres. Weatherford told the black students the college would help the accused find legal counsel, he said such counsel would be retained by the students and not by the college. After Pres. Weatherford left his office, several more black students occupied his office. Some brought blankets, books and playing cards. Various members of the college faculty and staff remained with the black students during the entire period of the occupation, Pres. Weatherford said. During the 22-hour period, the number of black students occupying Pres. Weatherford's office fluctuated between 20 and 80. Weatherford added that at no time did the college attempt to pressure city or county officials concerning the case.

The students remained in his office until noon the next day, Tuesday. At this time the students were told by Larry Greathouse, '63, who had been retained as attorney for the two accused students, that Gore and Summerville's case would not come up before the grand jury until Friday, March 6. Shortly after talking with Greathouse, the black students voluntarily left Pres. Weatherford's office.

At the hearing the grand jury dismissed the concealed deadly weapon charge against Gore on the grounds that Berea police had found the pistol on him only after an illegal search had been performed, Greathouse said. "No complaint had been received about Gore and there was not a sufficient cause to search him," Greathouse said.

The case against Summerville, who allegedly was carrying the club, was referred back to Berea Police Court as the

President Weatherford discusses grievances with students

charge was a misdemeanor, not a felony. Judge Noss had bound Summerville over to the grand jury thinking his court did not have jurisdiction in the matter, Greathouse said. In a preliminary hearing the next day, Judge Noss dismissed the charge against Summerville saying that if he had not, it would appear that carrying a club out in the open was a greater offense than carrying a concealed deadly weapon.

Pres. Weatherford looked upon the occupation of his office as a continuing conversation and not so much a violation of the college regulations. He said his decision not to invoke college discipline portrays an inclination on his part not to call in police or enforce the regulation against unauthorized occupation unless it is absolutely necessary. "Each incident has to be viewed separately and one incident cannot be used as a benchmark for future incidents," Pres. Weatherford added that the college regulation concerning unauthorized occupation is an important one and will be enforced when he deems it feasible and necessary.

Marshall said black students on campus viewed the occupation of Pres. Weatherford's office as a step forward in that they "were pretty well satisfied as to the way things were handled and gained faith in the administration and felt a sense of justice." He said he did not know if the black students who occupied Pres. Weatherford's office were aware of the possible disciplinary action which could be taken before the regulation was read to them. Marshall said he was not sure the black students understood the regulation concerning unauthorized occupation of buildings as it was "vague and unclear." Marshall said prior to the incident, he himself "had not even read the regulation." "If the president allowed the students to come into his office, the occupation could not be termed 'unauthorized,'" Marshall said.

"In terms of our feelings and espirit de corps among members of the campus community, we came out of the incident quite well," Pres. Weatherford said. "I don't guess one could interpret the incident as a step forward, but I don't feel the incident has created a rift in the campus community. In a sense we achieved a 'victory' in that we did not create breaches on campus and the incident was kept non-violent."

Page 11 of the same article in the May-June edition of <u>The Berea Alumnus</u> with a photograph showing President Weatherford discussing grievances with black students during the occupation of the President's Office in March 1970.[95]

---

[95]Courtesy Claudette Schmidt's Personal Scrapbook, 1968-72.

So the early risers among the Berea students were greeted by the picketers in front of Lincoln Hall. Most of the white students smiled in surprise. The passing black students asked a few questions and then joined the picket line. A group of black female students, led by Gay Nell Bell and Dorothy Osgood, even took the initiative and formed a second picket line in front of the Hutchins Library. Ms. Sarah Frior, who worked at the Library, and supervised some of the protesting women, came out and told them to: "Get in here and get to work, instead of walking around out here acting like monkeys." This only made the black women more determined to continue. Some came over and told us men what had happened, and since we had only recently enjoyed a great spaghetti dinner at Ms. Frior's home, several of us marched over and offered to pay her for our dinner, which she refused to accept.

President Willis Weatherford[96]

When President Weatherford arrived, he invited us inside to sit and talk. There were maybe 25 or more students gathered by then. President Weatherford handled the entire situation very well. He was already aware that the three young men had been arrested and promised to do what he could. He also inquired about other complaints, and he was told about Ms. Frior's remarks to the female students, which they felt were not only insulting but bordered on being racist.

President Weatherford told someone to go over and tell Ms. Frior to come see him. Ms. Frior came over visibly shaken and nervous about being called before the President. He asked us what should he do with her, and one black female student yelled: "Get rid of her!" I personally could not see us causing a middle-aged woman

[96]Photograph courtesy The Berea College Digital Collections, Berea Chimes Online, 1969, p. 24.

to lose her job when she was, in fact, a very kind hearted person, and probably did not realize the hurtfulness that she had caused. So I spoke up (and along with my girlfriend Claudette) said: "No don't fire her. Just tell her not to do it again." So Ms. Frior got the message and returned visibly shaken to the library. She remained friendly, however, to me, and seemingly to the black students who continued to work under her in the Library.[97]

Ms. Sarah Frior[98]

President Weatherford left us to occupy his office and promised to try to have the three young men released soon. As the day progressed, the number of black students occupying Lincoln Hall swelled, and classes were dismissed for the remainder of the day.

There seemed to be a general acknowledgment among the faculty and administrators that the black students' occupation had some merit, and that the three students should be released from jail as soon as possible. Some of the faculty realized that we "occupiers" had not eaten all day, so late in the evening, Professor Larry Lipchinsky and Dr. Matilda Cartledge arrived with sandwiches and sodas, which were hungrily gobbled down. The faculty's gesture of concern and food, went a long way toward easing the tensions because we now felt that the people who mattered on campus were indeed on our side.

---

[97]My girlfriend Claudette was among those who continued to work under Ms. Frior at the Library.
[98]Photograph courtesy The Berea College Digital Collections, Berea Chimes Online, 1968, p. 130.

Mr. Larry Lipchinsky[99]   Dr. Matilda Cartledge[100]

We occupied the building all night, sleeping on the floor, and in chairs. At one point, two of the upper-class female students who had joined the occupation, Eva Reed, and Savela Jackson, suggested that if I had any influence among the students, then I should remind some of the freshmen of the seriousness of our purpose. I immediately found the offending freshmen (one was drinking a bottle of whiskey) and chastised them for their poor conduct. In a big-brotherly fashion, I reminded them that we were not there to drink, party, and have fun, but to press for their fellow students' release. To their credit, from then on, the offending freshmen put on their best behavior.

The next morning, Mr. Marshall came over and informed us that the three young men would be released later in the morning and that we might want to come to the town hall to welcome them back as they were released. So we went downtown as a group and watched their release, and listened to some remarks from Judge George Noss, who was the Magistrate for the town. All of the charges were eventually dropped.

---

[99]Photograph courtesy The Berea College Digital Collections, Berea Chimes Online, 1970, p.80.
[100]Photograph courtesy The Berea College Digital Collections, Berea Chimes Online, 1966, p. 128.

Judge George Noss[101]

Unfortunately, the three young freshmen who were arrested were apparently not ready for a long-term commitment to Berea. At the end of the school year (June 1970), they left and did not return. My girlfriend, Claudette, and I, later saw Glen Gore in Washington, D.C., in about 1972, where I think he said that he had enrolled in Federal City College. Although he was from near Beckley, West Virginia, Glen often said at Berea that he spent most of the time in Washington, D.C., anyway.

"We Want Our Own Floor!"

Following the successful protest of the arrest of the three black freshmen, a group of freshmen black males, came up with the idea of getting as many black men as possible to live on the same floor in Dana Hall beginning in the Fall of 1970. They took their idea to Mr. Marshall in an attempt to get his support. Mr. Marshall was able to see through their plan, which was to allow themselves the opportunity to live in a modern dormitory, rather than remain in the older freshmen dorms of Blue Ridge or Pearsons, or the even much older sophomore dorm known as Howard Hall.

The group of black freshmen knew that the only way they would be able to live in Dana Hall would be for the current sophomore and junior men to sign them in as roommates. So their plan, in my opinion, was actually a scheme, rather than a sincere desire for brotherhood.

---

[101]Photograph courtesy The Berea College Digital Collections, Berea Chimes Online, 1965, p. 112.

Mr. Marshall, went along with the idea, as an impartial referee. He called a meeting of all of the black men and presented the idea. Mr. Marshall was skeptical of the freshmen's motives. He pointed out to the freshmen that they had stated that one of their desires was to have an all-black floor so that they could have an all-black intermural football team. Mr. Marshall reminded them, however, that most of the black sophomores and juniors were at a point in their college careers where they were not that interested in intermural football anymore.

A decision was finally reached by the sophomores and juniors present, when freshman, David Goins, arose and said that he knew that no one was going to sign him in any way. I immediately said: "Dave you can room with me." There was much laughter because David was known as an "early to bed (9 p.m.), early to rise (5 a.m.)" type of guy, and apparently everybody was surprised that I would so quickly ask him to be my roommate. The truth of the matter, was that of all of the freshmen guys, Dave, was a sincere small-town traditional black Berea student, and I knew that I would have very few problems getting along with him. The other upperclassmen who were present immediately began choosing roommates. Most of them, however, choose a roommate only on paper, and then eventually roomed with their favorite upper-class friend once the Fall term began. I did not change roommates, I signed Dave up and roomed with him until I graduated in December 1970.

David Goins[102]

---

[102]Photograph courtesy The Berea Digital Collections, <u>Berea Chimes Online</u>, 1970, p. 60.

VI

Two Crucial Elections: The BSU, Triumph, and Tragedy, Spring-Summer 1970

Prior to graduation exercises in the late Spring of 1970, the BSU elected it officers for the next school year. A sophomore (rising junior) Edsel Massey, was elected President. Edsel was quite talkative but liked by almost everyone. I cannot recall all of the four other elected officers, but I think I was again elected to one of the offices as a rising senior, along with Larry Robinson, a rising junior.

Edsel Massey, fourth President of the BSU.[103]

Student Body Presidential Election

In addition to the BSU elections, another more historic election occurred during the late Spring of 1970. My former roommate, rising senior Homer Williams, decided to run for Student Body President, a position (to the best of my knowledge), never before held by a black student. His challenger for the position was a friendly white rising senior, named Leonard Marr. A debate was set up for the two men in Phelps Stokes Chapel, where Homer turned in a very good performance. As we were leaving after the debate, Homer asked me: "How did I do Smith?" My simple answer was: "You won the debate, mate, hands down!"

---

[103]This photograph is from the <u>Berea College Yearbook, 1972</u> (volume is not online), p. 60. From the original volume, courtesy Claudette Schmidt's Personal Collection.

Leonard Marr[104] Homer Williams[105]

Homer also won the election, apparently rather easily, and was set to assume the Presidency in the Fall Semester of the 1970-71 school year. The truth of the matter was that Homer was very well liked, and had many friends, both black and white, and therefore had no problem gaining the white vote.

Homer and I had been I friends since our freshman year in Blue Ridge Hall. We had been roommates in Pearsons Hall during our sophomore year. We had served together as officers in the BSU. We had also attended a number of out of town college sponsored programs. For example, we attended the Little United Nations General Assembly at Indiana University in Bloomington, Indiana in the Spring of 1969; the Council of the Southern Mountains Conference in Fontana Village, North Carolina in the Spring of 1969; and the Chicago Theological Seminary Conference on Blacks in the Ministry in Fall of 1969. I had also accompanied Homer on a couple of trips when he worked for Mr. Bill Best and the Upward Bound Program. I assisted him in chaperoning the Upward Bound kids to Fontana Village, North Carolina in the Spring of 1969, and to the Cincinnati Reds baseball game in the late Spring of 1969. We also had worked together as "Students for Appalachia" from the Fall of 1969 through the Spring of 1970. I considered him my best buddy on campus, and I think most people who often saw us together also thought that we were best friends.

I was always amazed, however, at how many white friends Homer had. I think, for example, he was a much closer friend to my Blue Ridge roommate, Bob Montgomery than I was. When I later saw

[104]Photograph courtesy The Berea College Digital Collections, Berea Chimes Online, 1970, p. 47.
[105]Photograph courtesy The Berea College Digital Collections, Berea Chimes Online, 1970, p. 132.

Bob in 1982 (after 10 years), the first person he mentioned from our "school days" was Homer. When I later saw Dr. Marion Pride in 1985 (after many years), the first person she mentioned was Homer and the scholarship that had been created in his honor.

When Homer won the Student Body Presidency in the Spring of 1970, there were fewer than 125 black students out of a total student population of over 1500. There is no doubt that many of the white students knew him well, admired him, and voted for him.

The Death of Homer Williams

Homer, unfortunately, did not live to serve as Student Body President. He died in an automobile accident on September 2, 1970, only 5 days prior to his 21st birthday, and on the day that he was due to assume the Office of Student Body President, and address the incoming freshman class at Berea.

Homer Williams with fellow Berea student Jean Rockwell at the Washington Moratorium (anti-war rally), Nov. 15, 1969.[106]

---

[106]Photograph courtesy The Berea College Digital Collections, Berea Chimes Online, 1970, p. 132.

I had just returned to campus to register for the Fall Semester when I headed over to the Alumni Building and was met by senior Ronald Newkirk (Shaheed). Ron informed me that Edward de Rosset (Head of the Alumni Building) had just informed him that Homer had died that day. He had been killed when he apparently lost control of his father's pick-up truck. A young cousin riding with him had escaped injury. Ed de Rosset, apparently, had called Homer's home to find out why he had not arrived on campus to address the incoming freshman class and was given the sad news.

Ed de Rosset[107]

All who knew him were in shock. I was especially shocked, because I had seen him in Washington, D.C., only a few days earlier, where he was visiting relatives. Homer and I had gotten together with my brother Odell and his wife Linda from Baltimore, and we had picked up my girlfriend Claudette from her sisters' apartment in Washington and visited some people we knew in the city.[108] A day later, Homer and I had dinner with Claudette and her two sisters. The next day I left Washington for my home in South Carolina. Claudette informed me, that she and her sisters had Homer over a second time for dinner in Washington before he departed for his home in Stuarts Draft, Virginia.

Claudette said that she received the sad news when she arrived at the bus station in Knoxville, Tennessee in route back to Berea.

[107]Photograph courtesy The Berea College Digital Collections, <u>Berea Chimes Online</u>, 1968, p. 123.
[108]We visited with my cousin Rosa Gaffney Prysock; and with Donald Benson, a Berea student.

Isabelle Carpenter (Brummer) had arrived at the Knoxville bus station at about that time, from Swope, Virginia, which is very near Homer's hometown of Stuarts Draft. Isabelle gave Claudette the news and also informed Gay Nell Bell and Dorothy Osgood, two black seniors who were also in route to Berea.

I think the news was perhaps hardest on the black female seniors who had originally entered Berea with Homer in the Fall of 1967. The class had only a very small number of black students; only 5 males and 11 females. None of the 9 remaining black female seniors, who had entered Berea with Homer in 1967, attended his funeral. I have always believed that Homer was like a brother to them and they just could not bear attending.

In fact, of the 5 black males who entered Berea with Homer in 1967, I think only Donnie Buchanan and I attended the funeral. We also agreed to serve as pallbearers. The bulk of those attending the funeral were juniors (from the class that entered Berea in 1968). They probably saw Homer as simply a good friend.

Three automobile loads of students left Berea very early in the morning in order to arrive in Stuarts Draft, Virginia in time for the funeral. Mr. Marshall drove his car. Dr. Larry Ellis, a kind and generous white Professor of Physics, drove his van, and we borrowed one Berea College car.

The family seemed elated that we came. As I indicated earlier, a number of Berea men served as pallbearers. A number of Berea women also agreed to serve as flower bearers. We were fed dinner on the grounds of the family home following the funeral, and we left and drove through the night in order to get back to Berea for classes the following morning.

Memorials to Homer Williams

The Council of the Southern Mountains published an obituary in its magazine, <u>Mountain Life and Work</u>, soon after Homer's death. Homer and I had started the "Black Appalachian Commission" with the approval of the Council of the Southern Mountains, at its Fontana Village, North Carolina Conference in the Spring of 1969. Homer and I were surprised that the Council was so receptive to the idea. We were unable to accomplish much because the Council had very few funds, but as full-time students, we were able to hold a couple of Commission meetings that attracted the attention of persons living outside the Berea community. One of these persons was Carl E. Johnson, a community activist from Asheville, North Carolina, who was elected Chairman of the Commission.[109] The Black Commission continued to exist until the Council of the Southern Mountains, itself, ceased to exist in 1986.

Berea College also paid tribute to Homer's memory. On September 9, 1970, just seven days after his death, blacks and whites came together in a Memorial service for Homer. The campus minister, Reverend Randy Osborne, offered the Prayer. Expressions were made by Mr. Melvin Marshall. A Musical Selection was given by the Black Ensemble. Susan Smith gave a Reading, and Vickie Perdue delivered a Solo. Frederick de Rosset gave some Reflections, Francis Jackson gave some Reading Reflections, and the Black Ensemble gave a closing Musical Selection.

---

[109]For more on the Black Appalachian Commission see Appendix I.

CSM BOARD MEMBER
KILLED IN ACCIDENT

On September 2, Homer Williams, Jr., was killed when a pick-up truck he was driving went out of control near his home at Stuarts Draft, Va. Mr. Williams was a member of the Council of the Southern Mountains Board of Commissioners, representing the Black Appalachian Commission. He would have been a senior sociology student at Berea College this semester.

Homer was Acting President of the Berea College student body. He sang in the Black Ensemble and was active in the Black Student Union. He was deeply concerned about social issues and human problems. During the past year he worked with the Students for Appalachia (SFA) in the Richmond, Ky., black community.

Homer, one of eight children of Mr. and Mrs. Homer Williams, took a brief vacation between his summer work in SFA and the beginning of classes at Berea College to go home for the return of his brother from the Service. The accident occurred before his brother arrived.

There is no way to measure the loss of a life so full of promise. Perhaps the only fitting memorial is to work harder on the problems which were close to Homer's heart.

Memorial article on the death of Homer Williams in the Council of Southern Mountains' magazine, Mountain Life and Work, September 1970 issue.[110]

A MEMORIAL FOR

HOMER EDWARD WILLIAMS, JR.

SEPT. 7, 1949 - SEPT. 2, 1970

1:00 P.M., Sept. 9, 1970 - Phelps Stokes Chapel

Silent Meditation & Prayer------Randy Osborne

Expressions As We Remember----Melvin Marshall

Musical Selection---------------Black Ensemble
    "Let There Be Peace on Earth"

Reading Selection-----------------Susan Smith

Solo---------------------------------Vickie Perdue
    "Sometimes I Feel Like a Motherless Child'

Reflections------------------Fredrick deRosset

Reading Selection-------------Francis Jackson

Musical Selection---------------Black Ensemble
    'He's Sweet I Know'

Berea College Program for Memorial Service for Homer William, September 9, 1970.[111]

---

[111]Courtesy Claudette Schmidt's Personal Scrapbook, 1968-72.

Berea College also established the Homer E. William Memorial Scholarship Fund for Work in Interracial Education. The fund awarded a scholarship to two students (one black and one white) each year. Dr. Martha Pride, informed me in 1985, that each year when this scholarship was awarded, she would seek out the black and white recipients, and explain to them who Homer was and why this scholarship was created in his honor. For several years during the 1980s and early 1990s, I would request that my donations to the College go to the Homer E. Williams Memorial Scholarship Fund.

Dr. Martha Pride[112]

---

[112]Photograph courtesy The Berea College Digital Collections, <u>Berea Chimes Online</u>, 1966, p. 136.

VII

Gathered Together:
The BSU, Fall Semester 1970

So by the Fall of 1970, the Black Student Union had become fully solidified under the sponsorship of Mr. Marshall, and its president Edsel Massey. Although it had been a recognized student organization since the Spring of 1968, it had not been photographed as a group, for inclusion in the <u>Berea Chimes</u> yearbook. As the photograph below illustrates, the BSU was officially photographed for the first time in Fall of 1970 and appeared for the first time in the <u>Berea Chimes</u> in the Spring of 1971.

Members of the Black Student Union as photographed in the Alumni Building Lounge, Fall 1970. This was the first time the BSU was photographed as a group to appear in the <u>Berea Chimes</u>.[113]

The Incoming Freshmen Class of
September 1970

The incoming Berea freshman class of September 1970, that Homer Williams was scheduled to address as Student Body President, included only about 25 African American students, plus 5 students

---

[113]This photograph is from the <u>Berea College Yearbook, 1971</u> (volume is not online), p. 176. From the original volume, courtesy Claudette Schmidt's Personal Collection.

of color from Africa, and 2 from the Caribbean. Several were transfers, but most were freshmen. Unlike the year before, these young people were more typical of the traditional black and white Berea students. Most appeared to be from small towns and were rather soft-spoken, friendly, and easy to get along with. Marc Grigsby and his twin sister Martha Grigsby, from Elkins, West Virginia, were two members of this small class of incoming black freshmen who were very friendly and well-liked by everyone. Marc would later grant me a helpful interview that I would use in a senior research paper on "Blacks in Appalachia."

Living on the All-Black Floor

All in all, I would say that the experiment of living on an all-black[114] floor (Dana 4), turned out pretty well. Over the period of a semester, I think a "sense of brotherhood" did slowly develop. I provided, for example, haircuts (afro trims) at no charge to the sophomore guys, although my sophomore roommate, David Goins, who also cut hair, informed me that some were boasting of taking advantage of my generosity.[115]

There were some arguments, but generally, everyone got along pretty well. Most of the junior and senior guys went out of their way to get along with the sophomores (former freshmen), some of whom still showed a lack of maturity.

On one occasion, for example, two of the sophomore guys slipped women up to their room, and even into the showers. When they were detected, black guys lined up on both sides of the hallway outside their room and loudly berated them for slipping the two women onto our floor. The black men on the floor, in unison, made it clear to the two offending men that this was against college rules, and that they would not be allowed to embarrass our floor again.

The idea of a "winning" black intermural football team also did not work out very well primarily because of the immaturity of some

---

[114]In actuality, it was not completely an all-black floor. Two rooms remained unapplied for, so four white upperclassmen were able to sign up for those rooms. These guys were always friendly and got along well with the black guys.

[115]Dave rightfully insisted that the men should pay for haircuts, so some of his classmates ridiculed him by calling him a "black capitalist."

of the sophomores. Many of them refused to show up for practice. Charles Crowe, who had graduated at the end of the Spring Semester of 1970, and was now working as the college's black Admissions Recruiter, volunteered to serve as the coach of the Dana 4 team. In spite of Crowe's continued pleas, many of the sophomores, found excuses for not attending practices.

So in the first game of the season against either Howard 3 or Dana 1 (both had very good all-white teams),[116] the all-black Dana 4 team was embarrassingly defeated. One of the black sophomore guys even tried to pick a fight with one of the white guys because our team was losing so badly.

Some of the black guys evidently believed in the stereotype that blacks were naturally better athletes, and could win without practicing; although they saw the white team going to practice every day. After the first game, I excused myself and did not play anymore.

As I indicated earlier, however, there were positive sides to living on the all-black floor. I personally got to know some of the sophomore guys better, and the experience was beneficial. By living in close proximity, I was often able to engage some of them in meaningful dialogue. I would often talk to my roommate David Goins. In addition, since I was a night owl and studied late, I would often join sophomore David Frison in the study lounge of Dana Hall, because he too studied late at night. We would often break from studying and chat about our communities and our families.

I eventually interviewed three sophomores (my roommate David Goins, David Frison, and Robert "Lou" Williams) for a senior research paper on "Blacks in Appalachia."[117] All three were generous with their time, informing me about themselves, and about the small Black Appalachian communities that they grew up in. Dr. Richard Drake was very complimentary about the paper, so I was very appreciative of their help. In another class, entitled "Introduction to Political Science," I teamed up with sophomore Larry Grisby, who lived on the all-black floor, and was also enrolled in the course. We worked on a joint project together and both of us did well in the class.

---

[116]I think the first game of the season was against the team that always ran down onto the field with the Confederate Flag blowing in the breeze; and I'm pretty sure that team would have been Howard 3.

[117]As I indicated earlier, I also interviewed freshman Marc Grigsby for the research paper. In addition, I interviewed a junior, Vickie Perdue, and a black senior student, Donnie Buchanan.

So my overall experience of living on the all-black floor was in many ways positive. Most of the black men on the floor apparently felt that their experiences were also positive. So a tradition was established at Berea that school year (1970-1971) of black upper-class men living on an all-black floor or suite. This tradition was copied by the upper-class black women the following year when they managed to establish an all-black female suite in the brand new Kettering Hall.

Fond Memories and My Final Semester

I absolutely loved attending college. I enjoyed it so much that I managed (without trying hard) to attend three summers in a row. As indicated earlier, the first summer was spent in the Berea College Summer School, and the next two summers were spent at the Harvard Summer School, in its Harvard-Yale-Columbia Intensive Studies Program (ISSP).

So from the Fall of 1967 through the Fall of 1970, I was continually enrolled in college, with virtually no summer breaks. Because I was enjoying attending school year-round, I was rather surprised when I was informed by the Registrar's Office, around mid-semester, that I was scheduled to graduate at the end of December 1970.

I hustled over to the Registrar's Office to verify what they were saying, and lo and behold they were correct, I would indeed have enough credits to graduate at the end of December. I was also concerned about my status with the Selective Service Military Draft. I knew that some colleges and universities had stopped reporting the academic progress of their male students at the end of each semester, but I did not think Berea had reached that point yet. So I asked the black staff person (Mrs. Callie Dean) who worked in the Registrar's Office if they would have to report my progress to Selective Service. She said, "Oh yeah, we have to report it." So I decided there was nothing I could do but go ahead and graduate, then get a job during the upcoming Spring Semester and enter Graduate or Law School the following Fall.

So my final semester was extremely busy serving as a Teaching Assistant to Dr. Paul David Nelson, in the freshmen Issues and Values course, submitting applications to Graduate and Law

School, and staying on the Dean's List. My parents, grandmother, several younger siblings, and great-aunt attended my graduation, and some photographs were taken with President Weatherford. I stayed around and finished all of my packings, and left Berea a few days before Christmas in 1970, thus finishing my wonderful experience as a college student, and as a keen observer and active member of the BSU from the time of its founding.

My graduation in December 1970; from left, President Weatherford, myself, my great-aunt, Pearl Littlejohn.[118]

Epilogue: The BSU Legacy

Berea College has been unique among southern schools because of its nineteenth-century commitment to anti-slavery, and to interracial education. Because of that historic commitment, Berea acknowledged the repeal of the segregationist Day Law in Kentucky in 1950, and immediately admitted three black students.[119] Yet

[118]Courtesy Edward Smith's Personal Collection of Family Photographs.
[119]Gerald L. Smith, Karen Cotton McDaniel, John A. Hardin, eds. The Kentucky African American Encyclopedia. Lexington: The University Press of Kentucky, 2015, pp. 41-42.

seventeen years later (1967-68), the school's enrollment of over 1500 students included only 57 blacks.

As a student entering Berea in 1967, I had read (in the Berea College Bulletin), a brief history of the College's anti-slavery past, but that history had said little about its interracial past. There were no photographs of Carter G. Woodson (as there are now), or of other blacks from Berea's first experiment with racial integration.

So when I entered in 1967, I could see that Berea was ahead of other small southern colleges, like Wofford College and Converse College, in my hometown of Spartanburg, S.C., where almost no black students were enrolled. I reasoned, however, that Berea was ahead of those schools simply because it was not located in the Deep South, where the local opposition would have been stronger. Berea appeared to me in 1967 to be a school almost totally committed to Southern Appalachian white students.

The administration and faculty appeared, in fact, to be reluctant to acknowledge the college's interracial history, perhaps out of fear that the Trustees and Donors might object. It is also possible, however, that the administration and faculty may not have been fully aware of the college's interracial past. I didn't know, for example, until Dr. Paul David Nelson published an article in 1974, that the founder John G. Fee, and Second President Edward Fairchild, had consistently maintained a near racial balance of students at Berea during the college's first two decades.[120]

So by 1967-68, Berea's "black cultural" past had been either forgotten or hidden. Berea had become, as its founder John G. Fee had once warned, just another "mere white school." It had become, in the words of Fee, "no more than thousands of other schools in the South."[121]

So the accomplishments of the BSU during its first two years were remarkable, beginning with the simple acceptance and embrace of the word "black." For some black students, it was a severe psychological struggle to embrace a word with such negative meaning, and then give it a positive value.

The other accomplishments of the BSU were also amazing, such as the doubling of the black student population in just over one year; the hiring of the first black Counselor; the hiring of a

[120]Paul David Nelson, "Experiment in Interracial Education at Berea College, 1858–1908," Journal of Negro History 59 (Jan. 1974), p. 17.
[121]Ibid., p. 23.

black Admissions Recruiter; and the end of the infamous Star Lite Hike. In fact, all ten of the original BSU grievances were eventually addressed by the administration either in full or in part, during the period 1968-70.

The most important accomplishment, however, and the most lasting legacy of the BSU, was its re-introduction of "black culture" and history to Berea College. This was the primary objective of the BSU from the beginning, as was clearly stated in its Constitution.

As a BSU member and officer during the period 1968-70, I freely admit now, that I viewed the BSU as primarily a political organization, rather than a cultural one. I was more concerned with increasing the presence of black students and black faculty at Berea, and the eight other major complaints that the BSU initially lodged against the college.

I became involved in the cultural events, primarily because the female students (and especially my girlfriend, Claudette) were heavily involved. I tended to agree with Dr. James Holloway, that some of the faculty and administrators at Berea were only interested in "how we sang and dance." As long as the black students were happy singing and dancing, then race relations must be ok.

I now have a much broader appreciation for the impact of culture on society. Just as "black culture" has had a major impact on Berea College, thanks to the BSU; "black culture" has now become a dominant element in "American Popular Culture." The impact of blacks in music, dance, sports, and entertainment, has in fact put "black culture" into the mainstream of "American Popular Culture."

Changes in culture can have a more lasting impact on society than changes in politics. Politics, and especially periods of liberal political reform tend to move in thirty-year cycles. A period of reform is generally followed by a period of conservative reaction to those reforms.[122] Changes in culture, however, tend to be more long lasting. Ethnic foods that were once shunned, eventually become enjoyed by all. Ethnic music, song, dance, and even sports become accepted and embraced by all.

So the BSU succeeded overwhelmingly in its cultural objectives. Among the lasting cultural achievements of the organization today

---

[122]Arthur M. Schlesinger, Jr. The Cycles of American History. Boston: Houghton Mifflin Company, 1986, p. 45.

are the BSU itself, and the Miss BSU Pageant. The most prominent cultural monument to the organization today, however, is the now internationally renowned Black Music Ensemble, the roots of which were planted by those two freshmen BSU women (Eva Reed and Gay Nell Bell) in the Spring of 1968. May the BSU and the Black Music Ensemble live long, and continue to "increase," "stimulate," and "promote" black culture!

Appendix A

Envelope addressed to Edward Smith from Dr. Menefee of the Economic and Business Department, containing a Letter and the 8-page "Report of the Negro Studies Committee, September 23, 1968."[123]

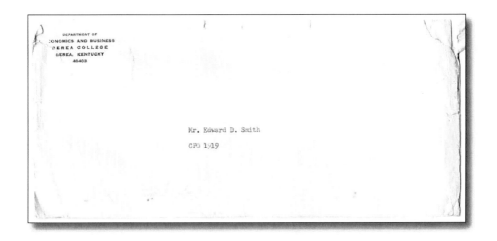

---

[123]This Envelope and the following Letter and 8-page Report, are courtesy Edward Smith's Personal Collection.

Box 2300
Berea College
Berea, Kentucky

September 23, 1968

President Willis D. Weatherford
Box 2317
Berea College

Dear President Weatherford:

Enclosed, at long last, is a report concerning the work of the Negro Studies Committee during the spring semester. The report is not signed by members of the Committee because I did the writing of it myself and did not think they should be held responsible for its wording. The entire Committee, however, devoted several meetings to the descriptions of the two new courses which are proposed. These proposals do represent complete and official Committee decisions, even as to language. The whole report, in outline form, was presented to the Committee before adjournment in May, and received general approval as to content. It is my intention that the substance of the enclosed report should faithfully represent this Committee concensus, with modifications only in wording, form, and arrangement.

You will note the Committee's recommendation that its work be continued during the 1968-69 school year and that work begin as early as possible in the fall. I am very sorry that this report to you was delayed until after school had opened, and I hope you can be more prompt in getting the Committee underway again if it is your decision to do so. Because I am to be on leave during the first semester, this report concludes my services as chairman of the Committee. It seems safe to assume that the appointment of a new chairman will considerably improve the efficiency of the Committee and expedite its work.

I want to express my genuine gratitude for the opportunity to serve with this Committee. Not only did the members give of their time and energies above and beyond the call of duty, but they participated with a depth of concern, a respect for difference, and a passion for truth which were truly inspiring. I have seldom had an experience from which I received so much, nor worked with a group for whom I have such respect.

Sincerely yours,

Robert G. Menefee

Robert G. Menefee
Chairman, 1967-68
Negro Studies Committee

cc: Dean Louis Smith

REPORT OF THE NEGRO STUDIES COMMITTEE

Part One: Membership and Activity

I. Membership

The Negro Studies Committee was appointed February 16, 1968 by President Willis D. Weatherford, Jr. He and Dean Louis Smith were ex officio members but met with the Committee only at the beginning. Other members appointed at that time were:

Faculty members: Matilda Cartledge
James Holloway
Emily Ann Smith
James Stermer
John White
Robert Menefee, Chairman

Student members: Ann Beard
Wallace Gatewood

Recognizing that its work would not be completed by June, the Committee asked that student membership be given continuity by the addition of two students who would not be graduating. On May 4, 1968, President Weatherford appointed the following students who attended the last two meetings of the Committee in May:

Susan Smith
Edward D. Smith

II. Meetings

The first meeting of the Negro Studies Committe was held February 22 with President Weatherford and Dean Smith. During the twelve working weeks remaining in the spring semester, the Committee held eleven meetings. Attendance usually numbered 6-8 members, and fell below 5 members on only one occasion. Meetings began at 4:30 and continued past 6:00 in nearly every case - one did not adjourn until almost 7:00.

The number and duration of meetings (especially during the spring semester) give some indication of the concern which members of the Negro Studies Committee brought to their work and of the effort devoted to it. Going beyond this, however, it should be noted that the discussions involved very wide philosophical differences and the deepest personal feelings of the members of the Committee. Under these circumstances, it would not have been surprising if the Committee had politely avoided the really tough issues and dealt only with superficial aspects, or, on the other hand, if the deep and intense differences had brought the Committee's work to a standstill and made significant conclusions impossible. That neither of these occurred is something of which the Committee members are, quite frankly, proud. Though every meeting of the Committee was strenuous, sometimes even painful, no one ceased to listen, to learn, and to participate.

III. Topics Considered

In a general way the subjects to which the Committee addressed itself may be

-2-

summarized as follows:

A. Questions of basic social philosophy and of attitudes toward people and contemporary events. These are fundamental to any curricular proposal.

B. The College curriculum and other aspects of the planned educational program. Here we identified three major areas of concern:

1. The General Education curriculum and other courses at the freshman/sophomore level.

2. Assemblies, chapels, conferences, special lectures, and visiting speakers.

3. Courses at the Senior College level.

C. The various types of materials available for learning, for teaching, and for research.

D. Suggestions for further work by the Committee, to be continued into the year 1968-69.

Part Two: Conclusions and Recommendations

I. The Negro Studies Committee reached agreement upon the following basic principles as a guide for its work and for the consideration of this topic by the entire faculty:

A. As a nation, as Christians, as a college, we face a crisis. We must begin with the recognition that this crisis arises, not from rioting and violence, but from the fact that God made of one blood and man has divided.

B. Berea's religious and educational commitments make it imperative that racism in all its forms be attacked by Christian witness and exposed by scientific analysis.

C. Whatever Berea is now doing in this regard is surely not sufficient for the time and the place.

D. Though problems are not solved by programs, neither are they solved without them. The importance of developing curricular and extra-curricular programs must not be minimized nor their implementation disparaged simply because, by themselves, they do not fulfill Berea's commitment.

II. The Committee should continue to function during the year 1968-69, with present members who are available and such others as the President shall appoint.

III. The Committee proposes that two courses be added to the curriculum at the advanced level so that the interested student can more adequately explore the

110

-3-

nature of the racial crisis in America.

A. Certain relevant courses are already available:

1. RACE AND INTERGROUP RELATIONS, Sociology 434, deals with the whole spectrum of minority groups and group relationships.

2. NEGRO HISTORY, History 373, will be offered for the first time in the fall of 1968.

3. CONTEMPORARY POLITICAL PHILOSOPHY, Philosophy/Political Science 333, recognizes that race relations have become the focus of major political and philosophical issues of our time.

B. The Negro Studies Committee proposes two additional courses at the junior/senior level. Descriptions of these proposed courses are attached. In connection with these proposals, it should be noted that:

1. The Committe strongly urges that the "issues" course (see the proposal for General Studies 389) be considered by the Curriculum Committee and presented to the College Faculty in the fall semester so that, if approved, it might be offered in the spring semester of 1968-69.

2. The Committee considers that a Negro teacher would have significant advantages in teaching these courses.

3. The Committee believes it important that these courses be interdisciplinary and carry the "general studies" designation.

IV. Along with the provision of curricular vehicles by which the interested student may probe more deeply, the Committee is most concerned that means be found by which to reach the entire student body. This need was underscored during the past school year by the polarization of student attitudes and the frequent expression of prejudice and hostility. As a beginning, the Committee presents these recommendations:

A. A new course should be designed and introduced at the freshman/sophomore level.

1. Such a course should be part of the required, General Education curriculum. Until that is feasible, it should be made available as an elective.

2. During its meetings in the spring, time did not permit the Committee to construct a proposal for the content of such a course. It is strongly recommended that this be a matter for early consideration by the Committee in the fall.

B. It is important that all those who teach required, General Education courses re-examine the content of those courses to be certain that topics related to race, prejudice, the ethics of intergroup relations, contemporary social conflict, etc., are receiving adequate attention.

-4-

This is not to suggest that such material should be introduced when irrelevant, but members of the Committee are convinced that much which is relevant has long been omitted. The President and/or the Academic Dean should raise this question especially with those who teach Psychology 102, History 103, General Studies 203, Bible 204, and Biology 205. The same or a similar question should be raised with respect to courses at all levels in every department, especially those in the Humanities and Social Sciences, or any other whose focus is the human being or human behavior.

C. College assemblies, conferences, concerts, lectureships, and visiting speakers should be utilized as important avenues of communication with the whole student body. Specific suggestions were submitted to the President, the chairman of the College Assembly Committee, and the Co-Ordinator of Religious Activities. Unfortunately, the suggestions were submitted quite late; it is hoped that the Negro Studies Committee will prepare such suggestions much earlier in the year 1968-69.

D. The Sunday night chapel services should include:

1. Worship services led by blacks as well as by whites.

2. Speakers who might help us think more deeply concerning the Christian commitment to brotherhood.

V. Available materials need to be inventoried and probably expanded.

A. We acknowledge with appreciation the work done by Mr. Drake, and by the students in Sociology 434 under the direction of Mr. Sterner. Since the Committee did not, in fact, make use of what had been prepared, further reference to this will appear in Part Three.

B. We urge that professional library staff be made available to prepare a recommendation regarding papers, periodicals, books, etc. (Miss Dorothy Crowder indicated an interest in working on this and has had considerable experience in the field). The cooperation of all members of the faculty should be solicited and utilized.

C. The Committee believes that library materials should, at a minimum, be adequate for general reading, for teaching the present and future courses referred to, and for undergraduate research in a wide variety of historical and contemporary topics.

D. The Audio-Visual Service holdings of films, filmstrips, and tapes related to Negro Studies need to be examined and probably expanded. An annotated list of both the rental and owned materials currently available on this topic would be very helpful to many teachers. Though A.V.S. might not be able to carry through this project with present staff, it does seem to be one in which the bulk of the work could be performed by carefully selected student labor.

VI. Contact should be made and ideas exchanged with off-campus consultants. We recommend that this be undertaken promptly in the fall with at least these objectives:

-5-

A. To examine related course offerings by quality colleges.

B. To provide guidance and/or critical evaluation regarding Berea's present offerings and proposed additions.

C. To explore other possible extra-curricular proposals (e.g., exchange of students and/or staff with Negro colleges).

D. To consider expansion of research potential through the sharing of materials, access to special collections, etc.

Part Three: Unfinished Business

It was recommended above that the Negro Studies Committee continue to function at least during the year 1968-69. As an aid to getting a prompt start, the Committee members felt that a summary of "unfinished business" would be useful. This list is in no sense intended to limit the future work of the Committee, only to facilitate it.

I. It seems important that the Committee continue to press for action with respect to:

A. Assemblies, chapels, visiting speakers, etc. Specific suggestions for the school year 1969-70 should be presented to appropriate officers and committees in October or November 1968, if possible.

B. Assuring that adequate attention is given this topic in existing courses. The President and/or Academic Dean should be asked to write teachers and departments as referred to in the recommendations above (See Part Two, Recommendation IV,B). If the Committee provided the President a proposed draft of a letter or letters, this would serve both to expedite matters and to utilize the thinking of the committee members regarding appropriate content.

C. First-semester consideration by the Curriculum Committee and then by the Faculty of the proposed course tentatively numbered and titled: "G.S. 389, Black and White Americans, Contemporary Issues". It is very much to be hoped that this course can be offered during the spring semester of the 1968-69 school year.

II. In its final report, the Committee on Appalachian Studies recommended that Berea adopt policy and procedure permitting students to construct Interdepartmental Majors. It seems appropriate that the Negro Studies Committee consider the usefulness of that proposal in the area of Negro Studies, and pass on to the President, the Dean, and the Curriculum Committee its conclusions.

III. If the Committee members continue to feel in the fall as they did in the spring, they will want to design and propose at least one course to be offered at the freshman or sophomore level in 1969-70. The question as to whether such a course would be required or elective will need to be considered in the light of the broader re-thinking of the General Education program planned for the 1968-69 school year.

113

-6-

IV. With the help of all those who are interested, the Committee should promote the expansion of available library materials. There were several suggestions as to how this might proceed:

A. Use should be made of two related projects which were undertaken during the spring of 1968:

1. Professor Stermer had the members of his Sociology 434 course search the library and prepare a list of materials now available.

2. Professor Drake referred us to an excellent annotated bibliography, "THE NEGRO IN THE UNITED STATES, A RESEARCH GUIDE" by Erwin K. Welsch. In preparation for the Negro History course which he will teach in the fall, Professor Drake had the library holdings checked against the Welsch listing and can provide information as to which of the items are now available here and which are not.

B. The cooperation of all interested faculty and students should be enlisted, specifically by asking any or all of them for bibliographical suggestions.

C. The major research centers for this topic could undoubtedly be helpful in suggesting the materials most essential for our purposes. One good suggestion was made by Professor Drake who gave us the name of Clifton H. Johnson, Director of Amistad Research Center, Fisk University.

D. As noted in the recommendations above, the total job of accumulating materials is going to require some paid time by a professional librarian. The Negro Studies Committee will undoubtedly need to press for a definite arrangement, budgeted funds, and may need to assist further in the process.

V. The Committee should work with the Director of Audio-Visual service on either or both of the following:

A. An expanded library of films, filmstrips, and tapes appropriate for Negro Studies.

B. Preparation and circulation of an annotated list of the materials available here or by rental. Such a list would also need to be kept up to date.

VI. Beginning promptly in the fall of 1968, the Committee's horizons should be expanded by visiting other schools, bringing consultants here, etc.

COURSES PROPOSED BY THE NEGRO STUDIES COMMITTEE

I.

G.S. 389: Black and White Americans, Contemporary Issues   (3 credits)

Purpose: The course will attempt to identify and examine systematically
the race-centered issues of American society. Students who take
this course should:

a. be made more aware of the issues

b. achieve a greater understanding of the causal forces at work

c. become more competent in dealing with the issues scientifically and ethically

Content: Certain issues seem to be basic, broad and continuing, e.g., the
nature of race, of racism, the role of law, of prejudice. Others
arise out of changing conditions or local concerns. The issues
to be studied should include central ones selected in advance
by the teacher/coordinator. These will give the course struc-
ture and make advance preparation possible. Other issues should
be selected by the students and teacher together so that the
students may have the experience of defining issues and, in
the process, keep the course timely and relevant.

Whatever the issues included, they should be examined in the
light of the best available research, knowledge and thinking.
The airing of diverse views and the expression of personal concerns should culminate in the discipline of scientific inquiry.

Organization: Directed by a teacher/coordinator who, in consultation with
the Dean and members of the class, will arrange to have consultants, lecturers, and contributors on the various topics. These
may be asked to:

a. suggest appropriate materials for assigned and supplementary
reading, and/or

b. meet one or more times with the class to deal with relevant
topics.

Typically such visiting participants would be Berea staff members,
but off-campus consultants and speakers should also be invited.
(A budget for this would need to be presented and approved in
advance.)

Eligibility: Junior-Senior classification or permission of instructor

II

G.S. 390: The American Negro, A Seminar   (2,3 credits)

Prerequisite: G.S. 389

Content: Each student is to prepare and present for class discussion
          a written report on a topic of his selection, the topic
          subject to approval by the:

          (a) Course teacher/coordinator

          (b) Chairman of appropriate department if the course is to
               be counted toward a major (see Credit below)

Eligibility: The course should be open only to Juniors and Seniors with
          a cumulative point standing of 2.5 or above, enrollment not
          to exceed 20 per section. If pre-registration exceeds that
          number and additional sections cannot be arranged, priority
          should be given to those registrants with highest point-
          standing and/or to seniors, subject to the discretion of the
          coordinator (with advice of the Dean and of students on cam-
          pus who have had the course previously). In the exercise of
          this discretion, the primary criteria would be interest in
          the course and ability to participate effectively in the
          seminar.

Credit: Within two weeks of final registration, a student who has en-
          rolled for G.S. 390 may apply to the appropriate department
          for permission to count this course as part of his major.
          The department chairman will confer with the student and the
          course-coordinator regarding the nature of the proposed
          report. If the chairman approves, the student may then
          officially register for the course with the name of the major
          as part of the course designation (e.g., Biology 390, History
          390, etc.)

Grading: A grade will be determined by the coordinator if G.S. credit
          only is involved. If credit is to be given toward a major,
          the written report will be graded by the coordinator, a mem-
          ber of the major department and a third person chosen by those
          two. The grade in the course will be determined principally
          by the quality of the written report, but effectiveness in
          class participation may also be considered. It will be the
          responsibility of the teacher/coordinator to see that the
          above procedure is implemented and an official grade reported
          to the Registrar.

Class report: Whenever, in the opinion of the coordinator and the Dean,
          (or a representative of his choosing) the class reports are of
          a quality and significance to warrant it, they shall be dupli-
          cated and made generally available. This might include any
          or all of the following:

                              Library copies
                              Sale on campus
                              Free distribution to interested persons
                              Other (?)

116

Appendix B

Envelope addressed to Ed Smith from Dr. John White of the Psychology Department, containing a Note and the 6-page "Spring 1969 Report of the Negro Studies Committee's Activities to Implement the Recommendations of the September 23, 1968, Report."[124]

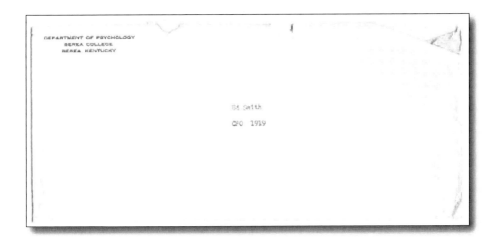

DEPARTMENT OF PSYCHOLOGY
BEREA COLLEGE
BEREA, KENTUCKY

Ed Smith

CPO 1919

---

[124]This Envelope and the following Note and 6-page Report, are courtesy Edward Smith's Personal Collection.

We as Britsts the opportunity to recognize Sarah's commitment
to interracial education and accept this task with humble recognition
of Sarah's past efforts. There is no doubt in our mind about the truth
represented in our Goal. It is our concern that we keep our commitment a
vital one, relevant to the current day. Thus, this report aims at
reassessing how we may implement our commitment but in no way seeks to
question its validity or relevance to all mankind.

[illegible]

I. [illegible]

[illegible]

Faculty Members: [illegible]
[illegible] - unable to attend second semester
Robert [illegible]
[illegible] Smith
[illegible] - unable to attend second semester
John White, Chairman

Student Members: Susan Smith
Edward Smith

II. Activities

A. Carrying out of Recommendations and Proposals of the Fall Report of the Committee
   1. Gained approval of G.S. 389: Black and White American Contemporary Issues by Curriculum Committee.
   2. Gained approval of G.S. 390: The American Negro, a Seminar to the Curriculum Committee in March. (See appendix A for course description of 389 and 390).
   3. Prepared recommendations to the Curriculum Committee concerning courses in the Required General Studies Curriculum.

B. New Recommendations and Activity
   1. A symposium presented by three Blacks who are actively involved in Human Rights or Community Development, to be held Tuesday afternoon and evening, 22 April 1969.
   2. The proposal of a 2-3 day Faculty Retreat to study our commitment to the Brotherhood of Man and how best to achieve it.
   3. A strong recommendation for increasing the number of Blacks on campus.

III. Conclusions and Recommendations

A. The Negro Studies Committee was quite pleased that the Curriculum Committee was able to approve G.S. 389. The effort put forth by the Administration in arranging for the course is also appreciated. We realize that the press of time made completely satisfactory arrangements most difficult, if not impossible.

We must note, however, that the current course does not carry out the description or catalog statement approved by the Curriculum Committee. Specifically we refer to the catalog statement: "An attempt to identify and examine systematically the race centered issues of American Society." And in the course description: "There are some issues that are basic and continuing such as the nature of race, the role of law, the nature of prejudice. These should be predetermined by the teacher/coordinator. Whatever the issues involved, they should be examined in the light of the best available [illegible]." We are pleased that [illegible] is being [illegible] [illegible] racial [illegible] to the teacher/coordinator [illegible] be allowed. This is in no way a slur on the current [illegible] as he took the course at the last minute request of the Administration and with some misgivings of his own.

B. A symposium was arranged for 20 April 1969. The speakers included:

Dr. James Hill, Ph.D.
Department of [Anthropology]
University of Kentucky Medical Center
Member of Lexington Human Rights Coalition

Julia Lewis
Civil Rights Leader
Lexington, Kentucky

Mark n Anne
Newport Community Action Commission
Newport, Kentucky   (Unable to attend)

All three speakers were Black and each had a different perspective on the problems of Blacks in Kentucky. A Tuesday afternoon convocation and Tuesday evening panel discussion were held.

C. Currently there are two courses that deal specifically with Negro Studies:

General Studies 399: Black and White American Contemporary Issues
Negro History 273

There are other courses such as the following which deal in varying degrees with problems related to the Negro in America:

G.S. 203: Introduction to Social Science
Sociology 432: Race and Intergroup Relations
Philosophy/Political Science 333: Contemporary Political Philosophy

We strongly recommend that G.S. 399: The American Negro, a Seminar as described in our 23 September 1969 report be implemented for next year (9/70 as it is the companion course of 399. For a description see appendix A.

D. Our tradition and commitments demand that we actively pursue the issues of brotherhood and racial understanding. It is essential that these issues be raised as soon as possible and continue to be raised throughout a student's academic career. The glaring lack in our current program is some form of academic contact that reaches all of our students early in their careers.

Currently, G.S. 203: Introduction to Social Science seems to be the only required course with specific race relations content. Regarding the objectives stated above, it has two shortcomings. First, it is offered at the 200 level and is rarely taken before the sophomore year, often is taken later. Second, the time devoted to race relations has dwindled from approximately 1/4 of the course (as of the early 1950's) to a week or less at the present time. To the Committee members this opens a tragic irony in view of contemporary social tensions.

As an interim measure it is urged that we return to the earlier policy in which 1/4 of the course is spent on the problem of race in America. As a final aim we definitely need some sort of the freshman curriculum to deal with the problem.

Our freshmen must be made aware that our concern with the brotherhood of man and interracial education is a non-elite one. One example of the Negro in America today well also seem to be the most relevant point of departure considering our tradition. Thus, realizing the limitations of any purely academic approach, the issues must still be raised somewhere in the freshman level required courses.

We hesitate to state specifically how, due to the curriculum study that is in progress. We do, however, feel a need to its capacity. It might be done through an interdisciplinary freshman seminar which could attempt to relate today's constituents to the contemporary world. In such a course the ethical, scientific, and social ramifications of race, the Appalachian region, the poor and the lack of brotherhood could be explored. Such an interdisciplinary course could involve all of the community is white, in our conditions. [...]

[...]

A profound [...] that collective awareness of our aims as the core of the faculty [...] but there are structural matters that limit this process [...] We refer to the difficulty of a busy staff in keeping up with the factual and emotional dimensions of the race problem. Most staff members cannot grasp the time for more research and the number of blacks on campus is not sufficient for us to learn from personal interaction alone.

As a beginning, we recommend two approaches to securing a more compelling intellectual and intuitive grasp of the problem:
1. A faculty retreat on current issues of race
2. Increasing the number of blacks on campus

(1) A faculty retreat could provide an opportunity for all of us to be better informed on the ethical, legal, economic and psychological dimensions of the problem. We could become more aware of the diversity of opinion and varieties of implementation, both in and out of our community. Such a joining together to review a greater awareness of our aims could not help producing greater cohesiveness and renewed effort on the part of the staff.

(2) Increasing the number of black members of our community would provide more opportunity for interaction on all levels. The social sciences have demonstrated that prejudice is effectively cancelled and mutual respect fostered by close and frequent interaction on an egalitarian basis. Certainly we desire that all our students, who come from socio-economic levels likely to be prejudiced, should have the opportunity to develop an open and Christian attitude in relation to race. Increasing the number of blacks will not solve the problems but it is certainly an essential step in the process.

It is therefore suggesting that we are by-passing a potent force for educating and liberating our total community. (Note: Increasing the number of blacks does not necessarily imply more high-risk students. There is evidence that we are not reaching all the blacks in our area that meet our current standards. It might ... to that end), increasing our recruiting efforts would be quite effective. However, we recognize various alternatives to increasing the number of blacks but feel the exploration of these alternatives to be beyond the original purpose of this committee.

COURSE

Department: [illegible]

Course: 374

Title: Black and White Americans, Contemporary Issues

Credit: 3

Lectures per week: 3 Contact hours a week

Laboratories per week: N.A.

Prerequisite: Junior-Senior standing or permission of Instructor

Catalog Statement: An attempt to identify and examine systematically the
race-centered issues of American society. Students who
take this course should:
a) be made more aware of the issues
b) achieve a greater understanding of the
causal forces at work
c) become more competent in dealing with the issues
scientifically and ethically.

Brief Description: There are some issues that are basic and continuing such as
the nature of race, the role of law, the nature of prejudice.
These should be predetermined by the teacher/coordinator.
Other issues due to changing conditions or local concerns
may be selected and studied by the students and teacher/coordinator
in the light of the best available research, knowledge and
thinking. The airing of diverse views and the expression of
personal concerns should culminate in the discipline of
scientific inquiry.
The course will be taught on a seminar basis with
appropriate consultants, lecturers, and contributors. The
Dean and students would be consulted in the selection of
outside contributors and a budget would need to be approved
in advance.

Offered: Once a year

Title: The American Negro, A Seminar

Credits: 3

Lectures per week: To be arranged

Laboratories per week: N. A.

Prerequisite: G.S. 389

Catalog Statement: This course is designed to allow students to continue study of problems areas developed in 389 in greater depth. Each student is to prepare and present for class discussion a written report of his selection. The topic is subject to approval by the:
    a. Course Coordinator
    b. Department Chairman if course is to be counted toward a major in that department.

Eligibility: The course should be open only to Juniors and Seniors with a cumulative point standing of 2.5 or above, enrollment not to exceed 20 per section. If pre-registration exceeds that number and additional sections cannot be arranged, priority should be given to those registrants with highest point standing and/or to seniors, subject to the discretion of the coordinator (with advice of the Dean and of students on campus who have had the course previously). In the exercise of this discretion, the primary criteria would be interest in the course and ability to participate effectively in the seminar.

Credit: Within two weeks of final registration, a student who has enrolled for G.S. 390 may apply to the appropriate department for permission to count this course as part of his major. The department chairman will confer with the student and the course-coordinator regarding the nature of the proposed report. If the chairman approves, the student may then officially register for the course with the name of the major as part of the course designation (e.g., Biology 390, History 390, etc.).

Grading: A grade will be determined by the coordinator if G.S. credit only is involved. If credit is to be given toward a major, the written report will be graded by the coordinator, a member of the major department and a third person chosen by those two. The grade in the course will be determined principally by the quality of the written report, but effectiveness in class participation may also be considered. It will be the responsibility of the teacher/coordinator to see that the above procedure is implemented and an official grade reported to the Registrar.

Class Report: Whenever, in the opinion of the coordinator and the Dean, (or a representative of his choosing) the class reports are of a quality and significance to warrant it, they shall be duplicated and made generally available. This might include any or all of the following:
    Library copies
    Sale on campus
    Free distribution to interested persons

Appendix C

Full Program for the "Amen Corner" at Talladega College, 1970.[125]

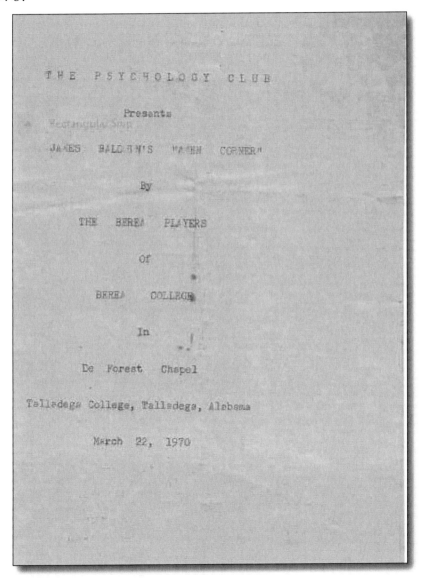

---

[125] Full Program (all 4 pages) are courtesy Claudette Schmidt's Personal Scrapbook, 1968-72.

125

THE   AMEN   CORNER

By James Baldwin

All the action takes place on a unit set
which is the church and home of Margaret Alexander

        Act   1 - A Sunday Morning in Harlem

        Act II - The Following Saturday
                    Morning

        Act III - The next morning

The Caste in Order of Appearance

Sister Margaret   Mary Palmer

 Sister Moore   Isabelle en Henderson

Sister Ida Jackson   Claudette Schmidt

Sister Odessa   Eva Reed

David (Margaret's son) Edsel Massey

Sister Boxer   Delphine Hopkins

Brother Boxer   David Prison

Luke (Margaret's Husband) Eugene Kelly

Sister Rice   Gay Nell Bell

Sister Douglas   Yuvonne Haynes

Sister Sally   Mildred Pearson

Songs from The Amen Corner

Act I

Song 1. Down at the Cross
Song 2. Everytime I feel the Spirit
Song 3. Gone to Jesus
Song 4 Glory, Glory, Hallelujah

Act III

Song 1 God be with You 'til We Meet again
Song 2 The Old Ship of Zion
Song 3 I'm going to sit at the Welcome Table
Song 4 Mr. Marshall solos with the Congrega-
        tion as they hum "Soon I will be
        done with the Trouble of the
        World"

Notes

The Amen Corner, is James Baldwin's first play.
He had just spent four years in Paris: "I
might live there forever and it would never be my home..
my home... to forget it would mean that my high
high pretentions were nothing but a fraud,
that the anguish of my forbears meant
nothing to me...

There certainly has not been enough progress
to solve Sister Margaret's dilemma: how to tre
treat her husband and her son as men and at
the same time to protect them from the
bloody consequences of trying to be a man
in this society...
Her triumph, which is also, if I may say so,
the historical triumph of the Negro people
in this country, is that she sees this finally
and accepts it, and, altho she has lost eve-
rything, also gains the keys of the Kingdom

From   Berea   College

Director   Paul Power

Music   Melvin Marshall

Technical Direction   Sharon Osolnik

                            Glen Miracle

Costumer   Benilda Atherly

Stage Manager   Drucilla Kelly

Talladega College Psychology Club

Publicity

    Dr. Clara C. Cooper
    Felicia Thomas
    Fredrika I. Bernard

Hospitality

    Lelia M. Sanders
    Shirley M. Grimmet
    Fredrika I. Bernard

Receptions

    Earnestine O'Neal
    Vonnie McLoyd
    Rita Simmons
    Mildred Tolson
    Anita Hamilton
    Mrs. Irene MacNair
Stage   Jerome Simmons, Kenneth Humphrey

Appendix D

Full Program for the very first concert given by the Black Ensemble on May 10, 1970, after which dinner was served at President Weatherford's home.[126]

[126] Full Program (all 4 pages) are courtesy Claudette Schmidt's Personal Scrapbook, 1968-72

Berea College's Black Ensemble

The Black Ensemble, on the Berea College campus, consists of approximately fifty members of the black student population. The members, being bound together by the common bond of a black heritage, are committed to Christian love and service. The group believes the singing of music rooted in the black culture and the Christian faith is one of the ways by which they can better identify with their culture, and yet fulfill the needs of their spiritual renewal. The repertoire of the Black Ensemble consists of semi-religious music, spirituals and gospel music and some dramatic interpretation.

Organized in September, 1969, as an outgrowth of the Black Student Union, the members of the Ensemble participate on a voluntary basis. Both accompanists and directors are also active members in the chorus. Today, the Ensemble is presented in CONCERT.

—o—

PHASE I — Spiritual

5 Choral - 1 Choral and Dramatic - 1 Solo - 1 Male Only

Interim:

Solo .... "Sometimes I Feel Like A Motherless Child" .... Miss Vickie Perdue

Selection .... Faith of Our Mothers Living Still .... Audience

PHASE II — Portrait of the Black Man

Narration .... "What Shall I Tell My Children Who Are Black?" ... Miss Susan Smith

Black Moods

The Black Anthem

PHASE III — Songs of HOPE - LOVE - PEACE - UNDERSTANDING

Interim:

Solo .... "The Theme From The Valley of The Dolls" ..... Miss Alfreda Turner

PHASE IV — SOUL GOSPEL

THE BLACK ENSEMBLE

Faculty Adviser-Director-Coordinator-Choreographer
Mr. Melvin L. Marshall

Student Coordinator	**Student Adviser-Director**
Mr. Charles D. Crowe	Miss Mary Willene Hairston
Accompanists	**Stage and Light Technicians**
Miss Elaine Wormley	Mr. Wayne E. Summerville
Miss Eleanor S. Hairston	Mr. William M. Turpin
Miss Gay N. Bell	Mr. Glen L. Gore
Miss Alfreda Turner	Mr. Alphonso C. Cotton
Drummers	**Artists**
Mr. William Churchill	Mr. Bruce Gray
Mr. Edsel J. Massey	Mr. Thomas A. Tucker

MEMBERSHIP

WOMEN

Name	Hometown and State	Voice Part
Askew, Linda	Talladega, Ala.	Soprano
*-Bell, Gay N.	Bessemer, Ala.	Alto
Carpenter, Isabelle	Swoope, Va.	Alto
Dean, Kathleen M.	Richmond, Ky.	Soprano
De'Shields, Manon	Chicago, Ill.	Alto
Garrison, Carrie	Seneca, S. C.	Alto
*-Hairston, Eleanor S.	Williamson, W. Va.	Alto
D-Hairston, Mary W.	Williamson, W. Va.	Soprano - Alto
Henderson, Ruthaleen	Oak Ridge, Tenn.	Alto
Hendrix, Carolyn	Birmingham, Ala	Soprano
Hopkins, Rita	Lynch, Kentucky	Alto
X-Howell, Pamela	Canton, No. C.	Soprano - Alto
Jackson, Narsie	Madison, Ala.	Soprano
Osgood, Dorothy	Midville, Ga.	Soprano
Palmer, Mary	Greenville, So. C.	Alto
S-Pearson, Mildred	Lincoln, Ala	Soprano - Alto
*S-Perdue, Vickie	Indianapolis, Ind.	Alto
*-Perry, Joyce	Westminister, So. C.	Alto
Rogers, Sharon	Greer, So. C.	Soprano
X-Schmidt, Claudette	Martinsville, Va.	Alto
*-Scott, Lydia	Pamplin, Va.	Soprano
O-Smith, Susan	Seneca, So. C.	Soprano
*SD-Turner, Alfreda	Richmond, Ky.	Soprano
*-Wormley, Elaine	Welch, West Va.	Alto
Young, Diane	Birmingham, Ala.	Soprano

*=Leads D=Directs S=Soloist X=Dramatist N=Narrator O=Orator

Membership Continued:

MEN

Name	Hometown and State	Voice Part
Buchanan, Donnie E.	Pineville, Ky.	Tenor
Burnside, Virgil	Stanford, Ky.	Bass
Churchill, William	Marion, Ky.	Bass
Crowe, Charles D.	Jonesboro, Tenn.	Tenor
Dennis, Robert L.	Birmingham, Ala.	Tenor
Findley, Alfonso	Liberia, West Africa	Bass
Foster, Billy B.	Greer, So. C.	Bass
X-Frison, David	Benham, Ky.	Bass
N-Fuller, Larry	Roebuck, So. C.	Tenor
Grisby, Larry	Athens, Ala.	Bass
Henderson, Michael	Greer, So. C.	Bass
O-Jackson, Francis	Richmond, Ky.	Bass
Jones, Marvin E.	Roanoke, Va.	Tenor
Kelly, Eugene	Asheville, No. C.	Bass
Lee, Ernest Wallace	Waynesville, No. C.	Tenor
Lewis, James	Somerset, Ky.	Tenor
*DN-Marshall, Melvin L.	Berea, Kentucky	Tenor
*D-Massey, Edsel	Leeds, Alabama	Tenor
Mitchell, Earl	Iuka, Mississippi	Tenor
Nutter, Robert	Bivalve, Md.	Bass
Patterson, Raymond	Louisville, Ky.	Tenor
Robertson, Larry D.	Washington, D. C.	Tenor
Scott, Ira E.	Knoxville, Tenn.	Tenor
Smith, Eddie D.	Spartanburg, So. C.	Tenor – Bass
Williams, Homer	Waynesboro, Va.	Bass

*=Leads D=Directs S=Soloist X=Dramatist N=Narrator O=Orator

The members of the Black Ensemble wish to express their thanks and appreciation to:

Ushers—From the Berea Community High School

Broaddus, Janice

Brown, Vickie

Dean, Eleanor

Marshall, Sybil Ann

Martin, Marilyn

Walker, Sarah

White, Jackie

Appendix E

"Little United Nations Assembly, 1968"

One of the things that I liked most about Berea, was that the college enabled me to attend a number of events and programs outside of the Berea College environment that opened my eyes to the larger world. The first such event occurred during the second semester of my Freshman Year, when I attended the "Little United Nations Assembly" (LUNA), at Indiana University, in Bloomington, Indiana. I went on the Berea College bus with other students (primarily History and Political Science majors), chaperoned by several faculty persons from the History Department. I believe the faculty escorts that year were Dr. Richard Drake, Dr. Frank Wray (who was a graduate of Indiana University), and Dr. Warren Lambert.

Dr. Warren Lambert[127]   Dr. Frank Wray[128]   Dr. Richard Drake[129]

I believe there were three black students onboard that year; and they were: Wallace Gatewood, a senior; Peggy Sloan, a junior; and myself. The other colleges did not have any blacks among their delegates.

---

[127]Photograph courtesy The Berea College Digital Collections, <u>Berea Chimes Online</u>, 1965, p. 106
[128]Photograph courtesy The Berea College Digital Collections, <u>Berea Chimes Online</u>, 1965, p. 113.
[129]Photograph courtesy The Berea College Digital Collections, <u>Berea Chimes Online</u>, 1965, p. 22.

Wallace Gatewood[130]   Peggy Sloan[131]   Edward Smith[132]

Among the busload of Berea white students who attended that year were three seniors whom I remember well: Betty Jean Hall, William Atwater, and Larry Wayne Bowman (who was also the Berea Student Body President).

Betty Jean Hall[133]   Willaim Awater[134]   Larry Wayne Bowman[135]

At that time, Indiana University was said to have over 40,000 students, so the physical size of the institution was astounding to me. Whenever I had to walk from one area of the 500,000 square feet Indiana Memorial Union building to another area, I would

[130]Photograph courtesy The Berea College Digital Collections, <u>Berea Chimes Online</u>, 1968, p. 29.

[131]Photograph courtesy The Berea College Digital Collections, <u>Berea Chimes Online</u>, 1969, p. 73.

[132]Photograph courtesy The Berea College Digital Collections, <u>Berea Chimes Online</u>, 1968, p. 65.

[133]Photograph courtesy The Berea College Digital Collections, <u>Berea Chimes Online</u>, 1968, p. 30

[134]Photograph courtesy The Berea College Digital Collections, <u>Berea Chimes Online</u>, 1968, p. 111.

[135]Photograph courtesy The Berea College Digital Collections, <u>Berea Chimes Online</u>, 1968, p. 23

always walk with someone who knew the way, so that I wouldn't get lost. There were students from numerous small colleges (primarily in Indiana), who along with the Berea students, represented most if not all of the countries that were members of the United Nations at that time. One of the first things I noticed was how "sharp" many of these students were, so after the Assembly ended, and I returned to Berea, I knew that I would have to brush up on my "Roberts Rules of Order."

My first visit to the Assembly, however, was not only interesting but exciting because it was influenced by the worldwide events happening during 1968. During this session of the Assembly, the Soviet Union was among the countries, represented by Berea students. As members of the Berea Soviet Delegation, we were influenced by the Cold War, the Colonial struggles, and the quest for civil rights in the United States.

Prior to going to the Assembly, I had written a protest article (some of which I plagiarized) entitled "A Letter From The Ghetto." The article was a denunciation of the United States Government for its treatment of blacks, and it ended by comparing the situation in America with "Apartheid" in South Africa. I signed the article "The Black Liberation Front," and submitted it to the college newspaper, the Pinnacle. I was surprised when the newspaper printed it in full and editorialized that the Berea Soviet Delegation planned to present the protest to the Little United Nations Assembly.

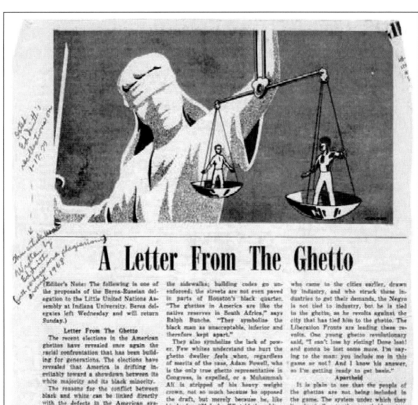

A Letter From The Ghetto

Newspaper article entitled "A Letter From The Ghetto" was written by me (Ed Smith) in the Spring of 1968, prior to the Little United Nations Assembly. The editor of the college newspaper, the <u>Pinnacle</u>, assumed that the Berea Soviet Delegation would present the protest letter to the Little United Nations Assembly.[136]

The former Merchant Marine, George McCalister, was among the Berea students representing the Soviets. George kept telling us Soviet delegates to remember that we were "old Bolsheviks." Another student would, of course, remind George that "this was not real" and that we were simply "play acting."

[136]Courtesy Edward Smith's Personal Collection.

At one point, however, we decided that the black members of the Berea Soviet Delegation, along with some of their white colleagues, would occupy the seats of the South African delegates, and claim them for the "Republic of Southwest Africa," which at that time was seeking independence from South Africa.

During a break, when the South African delegates were out of the Assembly Hall, we did occupy their seats and refused to give them up. The rancorous General Assembly then voted to unseat South Africa, throw it out of the Assembly, and give its seats to the brand new "Republic of Southwest Africa."

The exercise was lots of fun, but everyone was in agreement that this could not have happened in the real-world politics of the U.N. General Assembly in 1968. In fact, it would take 20 more years for South Africa to grant "Southwest Africa" its independence as the brand new nation of Namibia in 1988.

So during the 1968 session of the Little United Nations Assembly, the Berea students epitomized the historic spirit of Berea, as a forward-looking, justice seeking school, always a little ahead of public opinion in its region of the nation. The Berea students, in spontaneously creating the role of an unrecognized "Southwest Africa," were indeed looking into the future, and predicting the unfolding of events that would occur 20 years later.

Appendix F
"Little United Nations Assembly, 1969"

During the second semester of my Sophomore Year, I attended the "Little United Nations Assembly" (LUNA), at Indiana University, Bloomington, for the second year in a row. This time, the Berea College black student contingent again was made up of three students. They were Charlotte Beason, a junior; and Homer Williams, and myself, who were both sophomores. There was only one other black delegate from among all of the other colleges. So again Berea stood out for its exceptionalism in regards to racial equality. I'm sure that the other college delegates were well aware that Berea was apparently different

As in the previous year, we were accompanied by faculty chaperones. I think the faculty chaperones, this time, were: Dr. Richard Drake and Dr. Warren Lambert.

I was especially impressed by Charlotte Beason's knowledge and skill in parliamentary procedures at the 1969 session of the Assembly. She was elected by the entire Assembly to serve as Parliamentarian.

Appendix G

Harvard-Yale-Columbia ISSP, 1969"

During my Freshman Year, I learned to constantly check the bulletin board in the Alumni Building to catch notices or announcements of upcoming events and programs on and off campus. That is how I found out about the "Little United Nations Assembly." That is also how I found out about the Harvard-Yale-Columbia Intensive Studies Program (ISSP) during my Freshman Year.

When I saw the announcement on the bulletin board for the ISSP program for the following summer of 1969, I spoke to several seniors, as usual, to find out what they knew about the program. I spoke with Barbara Durr and I believe someone else, whom I can't recall now. They informed me that Barbara's boyfriend, John Fleming, who had graduated from Berea in 1966, had attended the program, and that I should apply.

Dr. Bradford (Brad) Crane, was the Berea College coordinator for the ISSP program, so I went to see him. He thought I would be a good candidate, so he too urged me to apply. So it turned out that I applied, along with two other black freshmen students, Rita Hopkins (Byrd), and Savela Jackson. All three of us were accepted into the program. I attended Harvard, and I think Rita attended Columbia, and Savela attended Yale or vice versa. Several white students were also accepted into the program for the summer of 1969: Roy Ladwig, William Boles, and Jean Rockwell attended Harvard with me.

Composite showing Berea students who attended The Harvard- Yale-Columbia Intensive Summer Studies Program (ISSP) in 1969. From left, Rita Hopkins, Jean Rockwell, Roy Ladwig, William Boles, and me (Ed Smith). Not pictured is **Savela Jackson**.[137]

---

[137]Photograph courtesy The Berea College Digital Collections, <u>Berea Chimes Online</u>, 1968, pp. 64-65; 1969, p. 14; and 1970, pp. 38, 44.

The summer of 1969 at Harvard was one of my most interesting collegiate experiences. Students from 35 southern colleges and universities attended the Harvard Summer School's Intensive Summer Studies Program (ISSP). Only eight predominately white colleges (Abilene Christian College of Texas, Berea, Berry College of Georgia, Lynchburg College of Virginia, Mercer University of Georgia, Millsaps College of Mississippi, Milligan College of Tennessee, and The University of Texas), were represented. So the program was mainly aimed at black students. This was the first time, since tenth grade, that I had been around a lot of black students. My room-mate was Richard Bell, a black student from Fort Valley State College, in Georgia. Richard was in a related program known as the Harvard University Summer School's Health Careers Program (HC), and he planned to become a medical doctor.

Although there was a sizable black student presence during the summer of 1969 on Harvard's campus, my intellectual contacts (there was very little time for socializing) remained fairly interracial, as they had been at Berea. During breaks in studying at night, my white Berean friend, Roy Ladwig, and I, would often get together with my black roommate Richard Bell, and a couple other black and white fellows, and go outside Harvard Yard to Harvard Square to have ham and eggs at 10 o'clock at night. During the day, after my morning Russian History Class, I would often eat lunch with fellow Berean Roy Ladwig and a number of white students.

Edward Smith with some of his classmates at Harvard, Summer of 1969. Roy Ladwig from Berea is in the brown shirt on the left.[138]

---

[138]Courtesy Edward Smith's Personal Collection of Photographs.

Harvard Summer School is where I learned to study real hard and love it. We were required to take a tutorial and one regular Harvard Summer School course. In 1969, my tutor was young Harvard Instructor, Dr. Angeliki Laiou, who would later become Head of the History Department, and the first woman to head a department at Harvard. She was one of the kindest, but also one of the most demanding professors, I have ever known. Very early in the tutorial when I was unable to complete what seemed like a ton of overnight assigned readings, she warned me kindly but firmly: "Edward smiling will get you nowhere!"

There were initially five students in our tutorial, Raines Whitfield from Virginia State College, Willi Ann Williams from Virginia Union College, Delores Jean Smith from Southern University, Mary Elcano from Lynchburg College, and me. By the end of the summer, however, only Mary Elcano and I were consistently showing up for class; although the others may have worked out some way to complete the course. The tutorial was on the "French Revolution." We really enjoyed Dr. Laiou's enthusiasm for teaching, and regretted when the class was over. I received an A-. Approximately a year and a half later I requested letters of recommendations from her. She informed me that she had gladly complied.

Greetings from Dr. Laiou informing me that she had written my Letters of Recommendations.[139]

My regular Harvard Summer School class in 1969 was in Russian History. It was taught by Dr. Edward Keenan. I had a little difficulty at first, but I met with him a time or two and did well on the exam. I received a B+.

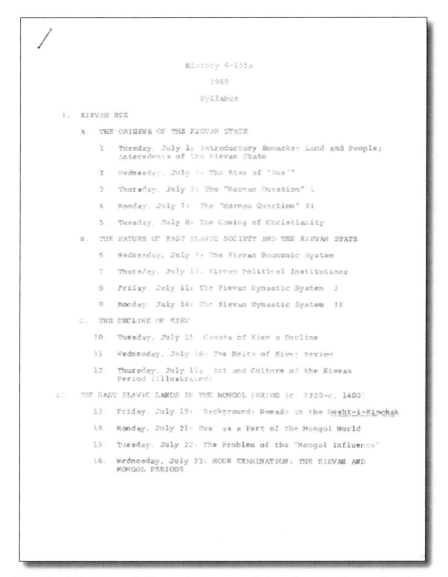

Page 1 of Dr. Edward Keenan's 4-page syllabus for the Kievan Russian class at Harvard, Summer 1969.[140]

---

[140]Courtesy Edward Smith's Personal Collection.

Most of the students in the 1969 Harvard ISSP were highly motivated, and most were looking forward to attending Graduate or Professional Schools. Grades were pretty important to most of the students, and most of us tried to make A's and B's.

The Harvard-Yale-Columbia Intensive Summer Studies Program (ISSP) also had a southern faculty component, known as the Faculty Audit Program (FAP). Select faculty members from the participating southern colleges attended the Summer School, where they audited courses. Dr. John Crowden, from Berea, attended the Harvard Summer School during the Summer of 1969. I would often pause outside the FAP dorm and chat with him and several other visiting faculty persons, since they were a number of years older than me, and seemed to be interested in chatting with the passing students. One day while we were chatting, Dr. Crowder, told me smilingly that his wife had informed him that the new black Counselor, had arrived at Berea with his family, and was "fitting in just fine;" he was "teaching Sunday School." The new Counselor was Mr. Melvin Marshall.

Appendix H

"Harvard-Yale-Columbia ISSP, 1970"

During the Summer of 1970, I attended the Harvard Summer School for the second straight year. I think the two other Berea black students who were accepted into ISSP the previous year, were again accepted and attended their respective schools during the Summer of 1970. I attended Harvard, and I think Rita Hopkins attended Columbia, and Savela Jackson attended Yale or vice versa. None of the white students (Roy Ladwig, William Boles, and Jean Rockwell) who had attended Harvard with me in 1969, returned in 1970. I assume they did not apply. I think that Jean Rockwell had already attended twice, so she probably did not apply to return in 1970. Dr. John Crowden also did not return to the Harvard Summer School Faculty Audit Program (FAP) in 1970. Dr. Abdul Rifai, of Berea's Political Science Department, however, did attend the Harvard Summer School FAP during the Summer of 1970.

During the Summer of 1970, students from only twenty-two Historic Black Colleges and Universities (HBCUs) attended the Harvard ISSP. The eight predominantly white southern colleges and universities from the previous summer, however, were again represented during the Summer of 1970. They again were: Abilene Christian College, Berea College, Berry College, Lynchburg College, Mercer University, Millsaps College, Milligan College, and The University of Texas. So, again the program was heavily aimed at black students. There were, however, slightly fewer students overall, this time around. I had a single room this summer, so I did not have a roommate.

As in the previous summer, although there was a sizable black student presence on Harvard's campus, my intellectual contacts (again there was very little time for socializing) remained fairly interracial, as they had been at Berea. My tutor was a young Harvard Instructor, Dr. Henry Binford. He was fairly easy-going, but his course on the History of Urban America was quite interesting. I think he had studied under the pioneering Harvard Urban Historian, Oscar Handling.

Like the previous summer, there were five students in my tutorial: They were: Lana Copeland from Berry College, Mary Elcano from Lynchburg College, Jane Shaw from Fisk University, David Willis from Mercer University, and me. I received an A-.

My regular Harvard Summer School class in 1970 was on the French Revolution. It was taught by the young French Historian, Dr. M. H. Abensour. He was pretty tough at first. On the first day of class, for example, he chastised Mary Elcano and me for arriving just a few minutes late for class. As time went on, however, he became very interested in my research on "The Question of the Blacks in the French Revolution." He told me that he knew that Napoleon was quite a schemer, but he was unaware that Napoleon had unsuccessfully schemed to win back Haiti. He liked my paper very much. I received an "A" in the course.

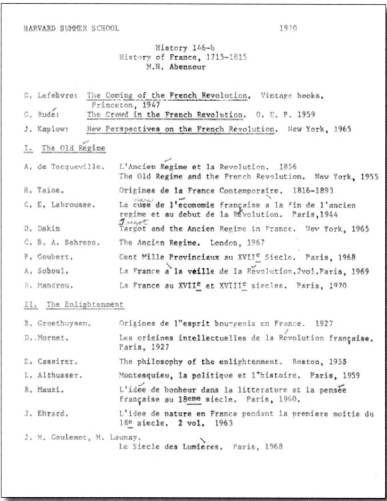

Page 1 of Professor Abensour's 6-page syllabus.[141]

---

[141]Courtesy Edward Smith's Personal Collection.

By the end of my second summer (1970) at Harvard, I had pretty much made up my mind that I would either attend Graduate School or perhaps Law School. I probably was aided in this decision by a number of black Berea graduates (former BSU members) who were attending professional schools in the Boston area.

At Harvard, I ran across Peggy Sloan, a 1969 Berea graduate, who had been accepted into the Harvard Law School. We chatted briefly in Harvard Yard.

Peggy Sloan[142]

During this summer, I also ran into Cathy Scott, who had also graduated from Berea in 1969 and was enrolled at Boston University as a graduate student in Spanish. We got together several times, and I would also sometimes run across her on her way to Harvard's Houghton Graduate Library. I think we also went to see the movie, "Cotton Comes to Harlem," which had just recently been released in May 1970, and was very popular that summer.

Catherine Scott[143]

---

[142]Photograph courtesy The Berea College Digital Collections, Berea Chimes Online, 1968, p. 51.
[143]Photograph courtesy The Berea College Digital Collections, Berea Chimes Online, 1969, p. 71.

Charles Crowe, who had just graduated from Berea in June 1970, and was working at a "camp" in New England for the summer, came down to Harvard one day looking for me. We got together and went over to visit with Cathy Scott.

Another Berea graduate, Frieda Hopkins (Outlaw), who had graduated in 1968, was also in Boston, where she and her husband were graduate students at Boston College. She invited Cathy Scott and me, over for dinner one evening, where I met her husband, and some of their friends.

Freida Hopkins Outlaw[144]

Freida, along with her husband, and her sister Rita Hopkins, also came by to visit me at Harvard near the end of the 1970 Summer School session. I think Rita had just finished the summer in either the Columbia or Yale ISSP Program and was visiting Freida before returning to Berea.

My girlfriend Claudette Schmidt was working in Washington, D.C., and staying with her two sisters during the Summer of 1970. She came up to visit me at Harvard one weekend. Mary Elcano's roommate lived in Boston and went home most weekends. So I arranged with the two of them to let Claudette room with Mary while her roommate was away for the weekend. Claudette and I had a nice time, looking around Cambridge and Boston.

At the end of the summer, I flew first to New York City, to visit my sister Juanita and her husband, Ernest Lee. Then I flew to Baltimore to visit my brother Odell and his wife Linda. I journeyed over to Washington, DC, with Odell and Linda, where I met up with Homer Williams, and visited with Claudette and her sisters, and saw Donald Benson, and my cousin Rosa Gaffney (Prysock). I

---

[144]Photograph courtesy The Berea College Digital Collections, Berea Chimes Online, 1968, p. 30.

left Baltimore's Friendship International Airport and flew home to Greenville-Spartanburg, S.C. Then I flew to Lexington Bluegrass Airport, took the airport shuttle to the Greyhound Bus Station, and then took the bus to Berea to begin my final semester at the college.

Appendix I

Envelope addressed to Edward Dean Smith from Carl E. Johnson, Black Commission, Council of the Southern Mountains, containing the 8-page Report of the Steering Committee of the Black Appalachian Commission (BAC) which met in Washington, D.C., on December 2nd and 3rd, 1970."[145]

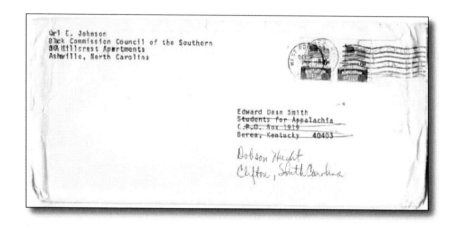

---

[145]This Envelope and the following 8-page report are courtesy Edward Smith's Personal Collection. I graduated at the end of December, 1970, so this was the last communication that I received from the Black Appalachian Commission.

FROM: CARL E. JOHNSON - CHAIRMAN,
BLACK APPALACHIAN COMMISSION.

TO: ALL MEMBERS OF THE BLACK
APPALACHIAN COMMISSION.

DATE: DECEMBER 9, 1970

This is a report of the Steering Committee, of the
Black Appalachian Commission which met in Washington, D.C.,
on December 2nd and 3rd, 1970, in the Conference Room of the
Black Women Community Development Foundation, Inc... And
at 4:00 p.m. on December 2, 1970, the Steering Committee
met with Ralph R. Widner, Executive Director of the
Appalachian Regional Commission, in his office at 1666
Connecticut Ave., N.W., Washington, D.C. Attending the
meeting along with the full Steering Committee, was representa-
tive from the Legal Defense and Educational Fund, The Southern
Education Foundation, The Southern Regional Council, The
Black Women Community Development Foundation, and Miss Ann Cora
Beard, of the Plymouth Settlement House, in Louisville,
Kentucky.

Following is a brief summary of the Steering Committee
meeting held on December 2, 1970, from 7 p.m. to 10:30, and
on December 3, from 9:00 a.m. to 3:30 p.m., in the Conference
Room of the Black Women Community Development Foundation:

I. The first order of business was to find a co-ordinator
to do a study of Black Appalachia. It was suggested that

151

-2-

Miss Ann Beard, who was present at the Conference, to be
Co-ordinator.

II. Jean Fairfax suggested that Legal Defense Fund could
provide some basic statistical data for us, and the following
outline of study was suggested:

1. Black population in Appalachia.

   a. Specific geographic location of Blacks, Rural
     and Urban.

   b. Where is the largest concentration of Blacks
     in the Appalachian States?

   c. Out migration (what percentage of young people
     leave Appalachia after high school).

2. Black Leadership

   a. Name and types of Black Organizations and whether
     or not they are providing adequate leadership.

   b. Non-organizational Black leaders (grass roots
     leaders).

3. Economic position of Blacks in Appalachia.

   a. Types of jobs - skilled or unskilled workers.

   b. Major social problems.

     1. What has happened after school desegregation?

     2. Number of Black families receiving public
       assistance.

     3. The size of the average family.

4. The types of Federal and State programs in the
   region by individual States.

   a. Are these programs accessible to the Blacks
     people in the region?

    b. What types of program are available for Black
        youths?

    c. Are there any Black leadership development
        programs for Black youth and adult?

  5. Housing for Blacks in Appalachia.

    a. Number of public housing units.

    b. Are the Federal Housing Assistance Program
        such as FHA and other Federal Housing Programs
        made unavailable to Blacks in the region?

    c. Are State Housing Programs available for Blacks?

  6. Registered Voters

    a. What percentage of Blacks are registered the
        region by individual States?

    b. Number of Blacks elected official to State and
        Local Government.

III. The main emphasis was to continue to focus on the Black leadership in Appalachia, and to unify the Black population around common grounds.

IV. It was suggested that a proposal be set out to receive funds for the operation of the Black Commission.

V. It was suggested that a deadline be set for locate information to find out where the Blacks are and set up a meeting for that particular purpose.

VI. Relation of Black Appalachian Commission and Council Southern Mountains have discussed, in assisting in

all phases - Remain in Council and do our independent funding.
Agreement written up with the Council-and write agreement
stating our position in the council.

VII. It was discussed that Black Women Community
Development Foundation be used as a conduit for funds;
Jean Fairfax gave us a brief history of the Black Women
Development Foundation and some of the things that they are
doing: Major project - Funding of Early Childhood Development
Program. Act mainly as a seed operation program - by trying
to help Black people get a better part of the action. Supports
organizations in Chicago and have someone in Africa looking
at community organizations.

VIII. It was suggested that we incorporate.
    a. What State to incorporate in?
    b. What should be the membership of the
       corporation?

IX. We should meet with CSM and set a transitional
project to pull the things together and to tell them what
we are going to do - And most of all play a key factor in
determining the status of Black Appalachia. It was discussed
whether or not our funds should go through the CSM? If we
incorporate we will be able to receive the funds.

It was suggested that we pull together, possibly in
March, 1971, a general overall meeting of the Black Leaders
in Appalachia.

-5-

The following Budget was suggested to get the Commission off the ground; and for the cost of a general leadership conference. This budget is based on a six (6) month period.

Cost

Steering Committee Meeting ------------ $ 1,500.00
   (two (2) meetings)

Salary for a Co-Ordinator ------------ 4,200.00

Travel ------------ 6,000.00

               Total $11,700.00

Administrative Cost

Office Rent ---------- $ 150.00
Phone ---------- 600.00
office material & Postage 1,000.00
part time secretary 1,500.00
   Total ----------- $3,250.00   3,250.00

General Leadership Conference
preliminary work of con. cost--10,000.00--10,000.00
cost of conference
mail order information
secretarial service

    TOTAL COST   ------------------ $24,950.00

Meeting With Appalachian Regional Commission:

It was suggested that the following basic questions be propounded to Ralph R. Weidner, executive director of the Commission:

1. Carl Johnson, Chairman of BAC will open the meeting - define BAC's purpose and what the organization intends to do.

2. Whether the Agency has ever done a specific study of Blacks in Appalachia? If so, when and what was the nature of the study?

3. What percentage of Blacks are employed at the agency level - stress the need to hire a Black person at the regional level.

4. Why are not more Black people involved at the local advisory board level, and the local staff.

5. Community Development:

    a. Economic Opportunity Requirement should be enforced by ARC.

    b. Blacks should participate in the new economic development.

    c. What has happened to the Blacks who have been replaced by the building of new highways? What is being done?

6. Education

    a. Does the ARC participate in Day Care Centers?

    b. What is ARC doing in Vocational Training Programs?

7. What type of Housing Programs is ARC building? Are Blacks involved either in living in the units or in the construction of them?

A full report of the outcome of the meeting with Ralph R. Weidner of the ARC will be forwarded to the members of the Black Appalachian Commission at a later date.

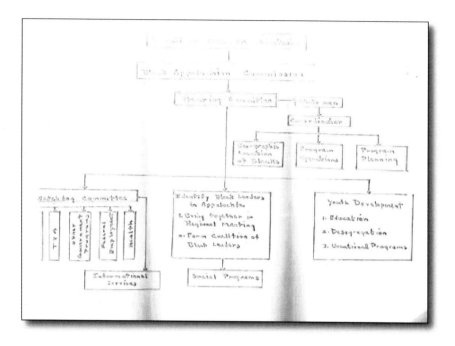

Appendix J

Envelope addressed to Edward D. Smith from Dean Joseph Taylor, Indiana University-Purdue University at Indianapolis, containing a letter dated March 29, 1971, regarding my interest in graduate schools and commenting on a vote by the Berea College Board of Trustees' (of which he had recently become a member) against an "Open Dorm Policy."[146]

---

[146]This Envelope and the following letter are courtesy Edward Smith's Personal Collection. This was my last communication with Dr. Taylor, whom I had gotten to know while a student at Berea. I remember him as being a friend of the Berea College BSU. On one occasion he addressed the BSU, after having driven from Indianapolis, in response to my invitation. In early 1970, he became the first black trustee of the college since James Bond, who served from 1896-1914. For his appointment as trustee see Jet Magazine, February 26, 1970, p. 48, or online at: https://books.google.com/books?id=TDkDAAAAMBAJ&pg=PA48&lpg=PA48&dq=Dr.+Joseph+Taylor,+Berea+College+Board+of+Trustees&source=bl&ots=x2go8a JEzr&sig=dSB4kiN1pKV3-o6PkSuaiĄMR_hk&hl=en&sa=X&ved=0ahUKEwiLuPfG_OHPAhXD5iYKHb4KCEsQ6AEIMzAD#v=onepage&q=Dr.%20Joseph%20 Taylor%2C%20Berea%20College%20Board%20of%20Trustees&f=false

INDIANA UNIVERSITY—PURDUE UNIVERSITY AT INDIANAPOLIS
Downtown Campus
421 WEST MICHIGAN STREET
INDIANAPOLIS, INDIANA 46202
317-264-7748

March 29, 1971

Mr. Edward D. Smith
4404 Old Frederick Road, Apt. F
Baltimore, Maryland 21229

Dear Ed:

Thanks for your letter. It was good to hear from you. I am glad that you have
decided to go to graduate school. Of course, we are delighted that you are thinking of coming this way. Let me recommend three things.

1) See if you can get a chance to talk with Doctor Benjamin Quarles
of the Morgan State College, Department of History. It would be
profitable to talk with him about your plans and get some advice
from him.

2) Write the Chairman of the Department of History at Indiana University, Bloomington, Indiana, 47401, for information about
graduate study next year.

3) Take the Graduate Records Examination if you have not already
done so.

I would be slow to leave a job if I were in a place where there is a reputable
educational institution. The languages and probably some beginning graduate work
you might be able to get at Morgan.

It was a blow to some students that the trustees voted against the Open Dorm Policy.
I trust that priorities will be re-ordered - by the students. Whatever the merits
of the students requests, I find it difficult to place open visitation at the top
of the list of things now needed at Berea. I look forward to some discussion when
we meet next month.

Best wishes. Let me hear from you as you take steps to continue your intellectual
growth.

Sincerely,

Joseph T. Taylor, Dean

JTT/vrb

Appendix K

(1)

November 26, 1967

We, the Black students of Berea College, are in
support of the iniation of a Negro History course in
the academic curriculum on this campus:

Catherine Scott
Geneva Isom
Daily Williams
Mercedes Washington
Marilyn Oliver
Pat Hodatt
Peggy Sloan
Barbara Durr
Ann Lora Beard
Julia M. Callier
Gay Nell Bell
Sylvester W. Cook

Jerry Harris
Charles Crowe
Tom Hutchins   Tarra Weatherly
Charlene Toiney
Donald Benson

It is my opinion that this interesting petition is a pre-BSU document. The initiative to create a "Negro History" course preceded the formation of the BSU and probably led to the appointment of the Negro Studies Committee by President Weatherford on February 14, 1968. The task of creating a "Negro History" course was taken on by Dr. Richard Drake, Chairman of the History Department. It appears (from Dr. Drake's correspondence), that the petition may have been submitted directly to him. He gained support from President Weatherford, and then sought advice from Dr. Joseph T. Taylor, Dean of the Indianapolis Campus of Indiana University. Dr. Drake introduced the course to a class of 37 students during the Fall Semester of 1968, which was the same time that the BSU was receiving greater recognition due to its chapel "walkout." So in his November 16, 1968, letter to Dr. Taylor, Dr. Drake rightfully linked the "Negro History" course to the then very vocal BSU organization, whose leaders were enrolled in the course. Dr. Drake's correspondence, along with this petition, however, might have led later researchers to assume that the BSU was in existence a year earlier, on November 26, 1967; but (according to memory) it was not officially organized until the early Spring Semester of 1968.[148]

I believe that this one-page petition (known in Special Collections as the signature page), is a pre-BSU document, because although it refers to Black students, it does not mention the BSU as an organization. It also refers to the older proper terminology of "Negro History," instead of the new emerging terminology of "Black History." Most importantly, the names of some of the leading individuals of the early BSU are missing from the petition. The name of Ken Miller, who issued the initial call for "all black students to meet" is missing from the document, as is the name of Wallace Gatewood, who was the first elected President of the BSU. Surely the President of the BSU would have provided his signature if the BSU had been existence at that time. The names of other senior activists, like Gwen Hale, Frieda Hopkins, and Sarah Wade are also missing from the list. In addition, the names of two juniors who would become officers of the organization in the Fall of 1968 (Odell Smith and Henry Smith) are also missing from the petition.

---

[148] See Shannon Wilson. Berea College: An Illustrated History. Lexington: The University of Kentucky Press, 2006, p. 166; or online at https:// books.google.com/books?id=U0PWalHC-rcC&pg=PA103&source=gbs_ toc_r&cad=3#v=onepage&q&f=false. See also Andrew Baskin. Berea College and Interracial Education: The First 150 Years-GSTR 210, Stage Four, or online at http://libraryguides.berea.edu/c.php?g=62507&p=402294. The petition and Dr. Drake's two related letters (dated July 6 and November 16, 1968) are located in the Berea College Archives, Record Group 6.24, Box 1, Folder1/1, Academic Divisions-History & Political Science, Afro-American Studies Program. Thanks to Sharyn Richards Mitchell of Special Collections & Archives, Hutchins Library, Berea College, for providing copies of the petition and of Dr. Drakes two letters to Dr. Taylor. The petition was received after this book was in production, so it has been attached as Appendix K.

Bibliography

Banks, James A, and Cherry A. Banks. March Toward Freedom: A History of Black Americans. Belmont, California: Lear Siegler, Inc./Fearon Publishers, 1974.

Baskin Andrew. Berea College and Interracial Education: The First 150 Years-GSTR 210, Stage Four, online at: http://libraryguides. berea.edu/c.php?g=62507&p=402294

Berea Carter G. Woodson Center, Video & Publications Library. "Selma-Montgomery 50th Year Celebration Reception in the Carter G. Woodson Center," at https://www.berea.edu/cgwc/video-library.

Berea College Library. Office of Special Collections. The Berea Digital Collections. The Berea Chimes Online, 1959-1970.

Berea College Library. Office of Special Collections. The Berea Digital Collections, Berea College History YouTube, 1970-71.

Connelly, Steven. "Racial Shooting in Berea on 1 Sep 1968." Berea Encyclopedia online blog, May 25, 2005. See this article at http:// bereaencyclopedia.blogspot.com/2005/05/racial-shooting-in-rea-on-1-sep-1968.html

Eblen, Tom. "50-years later, Berea alumni say Selma march changed their lives." Lexington, Kentucky Herald, February 15, 2015.

Ellis, Nomamdi. "Walking in the Footsteps of Peace: Forty Years of Civil Rights Marching." Berea, Kentucky: Berea College Magazine, Volume 75 (Spring 2005), pp. 16-24.

Fosl, Catherine, and Tracy E. K'Meyer. Freedom on the Border: An Oral History of the Civil Rights Movement in Kentucky (Lexington, Kentucky: The University of Kentucky Press, 2009; and online at: https://books.google.com/books?id=bnj0JHhoZ4oC&printsec=frontcover&source=gbs_ge_summary_r&cad=0#v=onepage&q&f=false

Franklin, John Hope. From Slavery to Freedom: A History of Negro Americans. 5th Edition, New York: Alfred A Knopf, 1980, pp. 481-482.

Grundy, Msiba Ann Beard. Interview with Msiba Ann Beard

Grundy, by Interviewer Margaret Brown. Louie B. Nunn Center for Oral History, University of Kentucky Libraries, Appalachia Oral History Collection, War On Poverty Oral History Project, June 5, 1991. Hear online at: https://nyx.uky.edu/oh/render.php?cachefile=1991oh187_app312_grundy_ohm.xml

Mack, Dwayne. "'Ain't Gonna Let Nobody Turn Me Around': Berea College's Participation in the Selma to Montgomery March." Cincinnati & Louisville: Ohio Valley History, Volume 5 (Spring 2005), pp. 43-62.

Nelson, Paul David. "Experiment in Interracial Education at Berea College, 1858–1908," Journal of Negro History 59 (Jan. 1974), pp. 13–27.

Schlesinger, Arthur M., Jr. The Cycles of American History. Boston: Houghton Mifflin Company, 1986, p. 45.

Smith, Claudette Schmidt. Claudette Schmidt Smith's Personal Collection of Schmidt Family Photographs.

Smith, Claudette Schmidt. Claudette Schmidt Smith's Personal Berea Scrapbook, 1968-72.

Smith, Edward D. Edward Smith's Personal Collection of Berea and Harvard Related Papers, and Photographs, 1968-1970.

Smith, Gerald L., Cotton, Karen McDaniel, and Hardin, John A. eds. The Kentucky African American Encyclopedia. Lexington: The University Press of Kentucky, 2015, pp. 41-42.

Whiting, Sam. "The Black Student Union at SFSU started it all," San Francisco Chronicle, February 1, 2010, and online at: http://www.sfgate.com/news/article/The-Black-Student-Union-at-SFSU-started-it-all-3274175.php

Wilson, Shannon Wilson. Berea College: An Illustrated History. Lexington: The University of Kentucky Press, 2006, p. 166; or online at: https://books.google.com/books?id=U0PWalHC-rcC&printsec=frontcover&source=gbs_ge_summary_r&cad=0#v=onepage&q&f=false

Index

Counselor (See also black Counselor): 64-65, 67

Crowden, (Dr.) John: attended Harvard ISSP Faculty Audit Program, 1969, 64

Crowe, Charles: JA Blue Ridge Hall, 31-32; mentioned 63n; together with Mr. Marshall formally organized Black Ensemble, 69; mentioned 76n; coached Dana 4 Team, 101

Dana Dorm: 28-29, 31, 82, 100-102

Dashikis: sewed by Geneva Isom and others for "Osun Dudu," 56

Day Law: black students prior to passage in 1904, 58; black students after repeal in 1950, 103

Dean, (Mrs.) Callie: hired in the Registrar's Office, Spring 1968, 49, 102

Dennis, Mary Palmer (See also Mary Palmer): 63, 70, 72

de Rosset, Edward ("Ed"): 90

de Rosset, Frederick ("Fred"): memorial program for Homer Williams, 92

Director of Admissions (Mr. Allan Morreim): 50-51, 65-67

Dixon, Shirley: elected sophomore class officer for 1968-1969, 36

Drake, (Dr.) Richard: marched in Montgomery, Alabama, 1965, 1n; debated increasing black enrollment, 52-54; complimentary about my research paper, 101

Duckett, Gay Nell Bell (See also Gay Nell Bell): initiated beginnings of Black Ensemble, 19, 55, 106; formed second picket line, 79; 91

Duckett, James: 76n

Durr, Barbara (See also Barbara Durr Fleming): 7n, 31

Eblen, Thomas (Tom): 2n

Edward Smith's Personal Collection: 14n, 15n, 16n, 17n, 21n, 38n, 93n

Edward Smith's Personal Collection of Family Photographs: 103n

English, (Dr.) Gary: 39, 42

Faculty Sponsor (See also BSU Sponsor): 11-13, 16, 34, 56-58; Mr. Marshall assumes role, 68

Female Students: majority of white freshmen (1967-68) were women, 36

Fleming, Barbara Durr (See also Barbara Durr): 7n, 31

Committee, 20-22; reported on Negro Studies Committee Meetings, 47

Hager, (Professor) Paul: proposed increasing black enrollment until "double" the national average, 52-54; head of Counseling and Testing, 52, 65

Hale, (Mr.) Leonard: response to Dr. Joseph Taylor's commencement speech, 1969, 58-59

Hamer, Fannie Lou: speaks at Berea, 34

Harris, Brenda Stuart (See also Brenda Stuart): led black freshmen on tour of campus, 55

Harris, (Dr.) Charles (M.D.): debates "color-blindness" with Dr. Holloway, 57-58

Harris, Jerry: marched in Montgomery, Alabama, 1965, 1, 1n, 2

Harris, Janice Maddox (See also Janice Maddox): JA Kentucky Hall, Fall 1968, 41-42

Harvard Summer School Faculty Audit Program (FAP): 64

Harvard-Yale-Columbia Intensive Summer Studies Program (ISSP): 64

Hill, Alice: JA Kentucky Hall, Fall 1968, 41

Hippies and Yippies: 42

historic black colleges: participating in ISSP 1969-1970, 64

History Department: Dr. Richard Drake, 52-54, 101

Holloway, (Dr.) James (See also Dr. Jim Holloway): first BSU Faculty Sponsor, 11-12; member Negro Studies Committee, 21-24; travels to Tennessee in the wake of King assassination, 30; invites John Lewis to Berea, 34-35; believes some faculty only interested in black "song and dance," 56-57; debates "color-blindness" with Dr. Harris, 57-58; his role assumed by Mr. Marshall, 68

Holloway, (Dr.) Jim (See also Dr. James Holloway): first BSU Faculty Sponsor, 11-12; member Negro Studies Committee, 21-24; travels to Tennessee in the wake of King assassination, 30; invites John Lewis to Berea, 34-35; believes some faculty only interested in black "song and dance," 56-57; debates "color-blindness" with Dr. Harris, 57-58; his role assumed by Mr. Marshall, 68

Hopkins, Freida (See also Freida Hopkins Outlaw): 7n

House, Cynthia Gaffney (See also Cynthia Gaffney): 65-66, 66n

Huff, Lanny: elected sophomore class officer for 1968-1969, 36

"Teaching Sunday School": reportedly Mr. Marshall was, 64

Tredennick, (Professor) Dorothy: debates increasing black enrollment, 52-54

Turpin, William: arrested, 75, 75n; arrest reported in The Berea Alumnus, 77-78; released, 81; did not return in the Fall, 82

University of Wisconsin, Madison: Dr. Okon Uya delivers tele-lecture from, 65, 65n

Upton, (Mrs.) Blanche: dorm mother, Kentucky Hall, 41-42

Uya, (Dr.) Okon: delivers tele-lecture course in African History from Wisconsin, 65, 65n

Walker, (Mrs.) Amanda: worked in the Food Service Kitchen, 50

"Walkout": by black students, Fall 1968, 47-49

Washington, D.C.: black students with connections to, 66, 75n; photograph of Homer Williams at Washington Moratorium 1969, 89; visiting with Homer Williams in Washington, Summer 1970, 90; spoke with Glen Gore in Washington DC in about 1972, 82.

Weatherford, (President) Willis: very well-liked, 10; use of the term "Niggra," 10, 47; appoints Negro Studies Committee, 20-22; ex officio member of Negro Studies Committee, 21; cancels classes for MLK funeral, 33; debates increasing black enrollment, 52-54; dinner at his home, 73; his office "occupied," 77-81; graduation photograph taken with, 103

White, (Dr.) John: member of Negro Studies Committee, 21-22

White Female Students: 10, 10n, 31, 36, 46, 46n

Williams, Dailey (See also Dailey William Smith): led black freshmen on hike of campus, 55

Williams, Homer: 9n; informed me of King Assassination, 30, 32-33; our campaign signs burned, 35; elected BSU officer, 63; elected Student Body President, 87-89; the death of, 89-91; memorials to, 91-95; scheduled to address freshmen, 99

Williams, Robert "Lou": interviewed for research paper on Blacks in Appalachia, 101

Woodie, (Dr.) Norris: debates increasing black enrollment, 52-54

Woodson, Carter G.: not mentioned in Berea literature in 1967, 104

Yoruba, ("Osun Dudu"): 56

Index to Appendices
(The Main Index to the book appears on pages 165-176)

180517-50-2-60W